The Toffs in the Tenement

By

Ron Windward

"Just loved this book, so many laugh out loud moments and made me smile often. It gives a wonderfully atmospheric feel for life in the tenements of 1960's Glasgow and the author has a way of serving up the hardship aspect with a particularly incisive wit, capturing that wonderful Glasgow humour perfectly. The characters are warm and likeable and draw you into their lives making you really care about what happens to them so much that I find myself looking forward to the next offering from Mr Windward."

Amazon review of Toffs in the Tenement

Toffs in the Tenement

First published in Great Britain in 2011 by Flesher Haugh Publishing

ISBN 978-1-4466-6568-8

Printed and bound through Lulu Publishing in the UK

Website: www.toffsinthetenement.co.uk
Publisher: Fleshers Haugh Publishing

Fleshers Haugh policy is to use papers that are natural, renewable and recyclable products and are made from wood grown in sustainable forests.
The logging and manufacturing processes are expected to conform to the enviromental regulations of the country of origin.

Available to buy from:

The Peoples Palace Museum on Glasgow Green

www.lulu.com	download or paperback
www.amazon.co.uk	download or paperback
www.amazon.com	download or paperback

Toffs in the Tenement

To everyone who survived the tenements....

Toffs in the Tenement

Contents

Available soon   **The Toffs in the Towerblock**

Enjoy a nostalgic trip back in time to the tenements of Heron St, Bridgeton in 1968, when kids made their own entertainment and every toy didn't need a battery.
When the sun seemed to shine for 8 weeks of the school summer holiday, and you wouldn't dream of giving any cheek to an adult in fear of a kick up the backside.
When everyone could leave their front door open, because they never had anything worth stealing, were everyone was in the same boat, struggling to make ends meet and living for a Friday (Payday).
When neighbours helped neighbours through trying times of poverty and hardship, and lifelong friendships were forged.

Toffs in the Tenement

Translation for Toffs

Minging	Smelly
Narket	Stop it
Fankle/Fankled	Twisted and mixed up
Clatty	Dirty
Manky	Dirty
The Shows'	The Carnival
The Steamie	Place to wash clothes
The Barra's	Outdoor Market
The Booly	Waste ground used for play
Bools / Jorries	Marbles
Stank	Drain Cover
A Close	Entrance to flats
Cludgie	Outside shared toilet
Sidey	2 teams playing football
The Minors	Saturday cinema for kids
Single End	One room flat
Midden	Dustbin
Lucky Midden	Dustbin behind shops
Furra	For a
Geeza	Give me
Gonny	Going to
Gon'	Going
Whit fur	What for
Wisnae	Wasn't
Wiz	Was
Urny'	Are not
Aye a 'um	Yes I am
Roon ra' back	Going round the backcourt
Geeza Brek	Cut me some slack

THE TOFFS IN THE TENEMENT

Introducing the Nairns
The year is 1968

*11 year old **Rupert Nairn** has spent the last two years living and going to school in Brigton (Bridgeton), Glasgow, private school educated until he was 9 years old, he now lives in a tenement (single end) with his family. He is highly intelligent, polite, observant and sensible, THIS IS HIS STORY..............*

***Father Hubert was a bank manager,** just like his dad before him, until he lost everything when money went missing at his bank, now he is employed as a shop assistant in the menswear department of a large store in Glasgow city centre called Arnott and Simpsons. Swapping their big house in the West end of Glasgow for a rented single end in Brigton; he is convinced he can be successful again. He has adapted quite well to his new life and makes an effort to fit in with the neighbours.*

***Mother Clarissa** hates the fact they have no money, and still clings on to her past snobbish life any little way she can, She has adapted to her new surroundings the best she can, but still firmly believes she is better than all her neighbours even though she was born and raised in a tenement in Partick until she married Hubert .A fact that comes to light now and again when she lets her guard down.*

***14 year old Wilhelmina** is Rupert's 'big sister, she hates her flat, her brother, her school, her life and most off all her dad for bringing her to Brigton, she hasn't adapted well to her new surroundings and is a mini version of her mother.......Oh! She also hates when, to annoy her, people call her Wullie Instead of Wilhelmina.*

Meet 'ra Nairn's

Thank God it's Friday, I thought as I pull my school cap out of my bag and place it on my head, Mother insists on me wearing it, the fact I am the only boy in school with a cap doesn't seem to bother her, I am probably the only boy in Bridgeton who wears a uniform to school.

As I turn into Heron St, another week of school finished, two whole days off to enjoy myself and pocket money to look forward to, I start to plan my weekend, my thoughts are interupted as I pass the first close in Heron St. "Haw Rupert, how Ur ye son?" shouts Mrs McKay from her ground floor window." Hi Mrs Mc Kay, I'm fine thank you", I reply. Mrs Mc Kay is a rather portly lady who just sits at that window all day every day; her arms on the window ledge are hidden by her enormous chest. She watches everything that happens in Heron St and even eats her dinner at the window. I think there must be a commode there as well because she never moves in case she misses anything.

"I saw yer maw wi a cupla' a big bags fae Marks and Spencer ra' day". "She must huv been in ra' toon", she announced,"Oh right", I say as I look back. If only she knew my mother took two empty Marks and Spencer bags with her when she is shopping, but shops in the Krazy House and puts her stuff in the Marks and Spencer bags to show off.

Toffs in the Tenement

I start to think how Heron St bustled on a sunny day, especially a Friday when all the men get paid. I could see my close ahead and the McCabe twins were playing marbles on a stank outside the close. Jamie and John were 10 years old and always had clothes that were a couple a sizes too big. They took great delight in telling anyone that would listen that they got their clothes from "the Meanie". They didn't have a clue what the Meanie was, and neither did I, but it must be okay if they gave you clothes for nothing. .

Between me and the McCabe twins was old Mr Mc Kay, slightly drunk, no, extremely drunk, he was trying his best to make it home from the Dog Leg pub on the corner of Heron St, a journey of about 100 yards that will take him the best part of an hour to make. "Awright son!" he shouts, "dae ye want a chip?" I quite like chips but on this occasion I politely declined. "Go' on take a chip", he insists, as I try to take a chip his hand is swaying all over the place with the bag of chips. I think if I take one it might upset his delicate balance and send him crashing to the ground. "No thanks", I say. "I was talking to Mrs Mc Kay a minute ago", I proclaim, trying to change the subject from soggy cold chips. "Oh wur ye noo?" he says, trying to straighten himself up. "Ah' huvnae spoke to her fur 18 months ye know." "Why's that?" I asked curiously. "Cos I don't like tae interrupt her", he says, laughing like an asthmatic seal.

He is still laughing to himself when I turn around just before I reach my close, only he has settled himself down on the pavement, chips on his lap and is struggling to get the lid off a quarter bottle of whisky. When he succeeds, he toasts invisible pals raising the bottle in the air, before gulping down half the contents as if it was lemonade.

"Dae ye want a game of bools, Roooopirt?" Jamie asks as I reach the close, "Ah'll play you furra steely", he continues. "I don't have my marbles with me", I inform him, and as soon as the words left my lips I knew what was coming. *"Ooooooohh! I don't have my marbles with me"*, they say together in a mock posh voice. "Its bools, or jorries ya diddy", says Jamie, "they only say marbles in the beano ya clown", says John. I tell them I will go up to the house and come back with my "bools" and hastily head in the close.

As soon as I enter the close the first thing to hit me was the smell. It's a mixture of damp, urine and bleach. Mrs Campbell, who stays on the same landing as me on the first floor, was just finishing her turn of the stairs. "Watch yer feet there noo!" she snipes, I felt like staring at my shoes for a laugh, but she would have just slapped me. "They stairs ur stull wet", she warns me in such a way as to suggest that if I put one foot on them I will be hung drawn and quartered. "I am just going round the back", I say sheepishly, and wait until she goes back into her house, I then run up the stairs two at a time. Half way up I fly past Mr Campbell going into the toilet with a newspaper under his arm, three families shared this outside toilet on a small landing halfway down the stairs. "Haw you, ya wee shite!" he bellows, "haw Ina, that wee posh bugger next door has stood oan yer clean stairs!" he shouts to his wife. "Whit, she screams, wait tae ah get ma hons oan ye ya wee bastard, efter me warning him anaw!" I couldn't help thinking how Mr Campbell must have floated down to the toilet on the landing so he didn't stand on the clean stairs..., before Mrs Campbell could exact any punishment I was up the stairs in a flash to the safety of our single end.

"Good afternoon mother", I shout as I enter the flat, maw, mum or as the other kids say mammy isn't allowed in our house, you see two years ago we stayed in the West end of Glasgow in a four bedroom detached house, Mother would visit friends for tea and scones, attend functions and have dinner parties at home, she was seriously posh. Father was a bank manager until something happened at the bank and we lost our home and money, he now works in a shop in the town, "Good afternoon Rupert", she replies "Did you have a nice day at school?" she continues, "Yes mother I had a lovely day", I say, "We are learning about something called decimalisation which is going to be introduced soon, it is very easy to learn as it is all in multiples of ten,....", she isn't listening to a word I am saying, choosing instead to fluff curtains covering the bed recess where me and my sister sleep. "Do you like them?", she asks, Now I can tell you anything about maths , physics, literature or history, but curtains, that's a bit like asking Einstein what horse won the 3.30 at Hamilton.

"They are very flowery", I offer feebly in response, "Do you think your father will like them ?", she asks , lets see, I think to myself, a guy who has lost all his money, home, status and friends and is now living in a single end in Bridgeton, "I'm sure father will love them" , I say sardonically. "Jolly good, jolly good", she says like Julie Andrews in Mary Poppins, now if she starts singing "Just a spoonful of sugar" I'm off.

Through the open window I can hear another bus rumbling up the street heading for the bus garage in Fordnuek St, down at the close I can also hear Jamie and John shouting, "Hullawrer Wullie, geeza kiss!", just to clarify, they aren't declaring their intention to come out the closet, so to speak, they were talking to my sister Wilhelmina, who everyone calls Wullie simply because they know it annoys her. "I wouldn't kiss you in case I got scabies", she retorts. I have often wondered what scabies are, is it a mixture of scabs and rabies, I don't know.., as I am getting changed behind mother's new curtains I can hear the front door open and slam shut, "I hate it here Mother!", Wilhelmina declares in a half sobbing manner, "I hate this flat, I hate this street, I hate......", " would you like to go shopping in the west end with me tomorrow?" , Mother interrupts. "Ok Wilhelmina replies calmly before flinging open the curtains of the bed recess, there I am, one leg in my trousers precariously balanced on a bed trying to get changed, I am now providing entertainment for the whole top deck of a full bus passing by outside our window.

Mother closes the curtains thank goodness, just before Mrs Campbell waltzes straight in to the flat and declares, "That's two bob ye owe me fur takin' yer turn a' the stairs Mrs Nairn...", I wonder why nobody uses first names..I think to myself as I listen from behind the curtains, "Can you wait until my husband comes in Mrs Campbell as I don't seem to have any change", Mother answers...., any change she might have had was now hanging outside our bed recess... "Aye, awright then ah'll cum back at hauf six afore ah go tae ra bingo", says Mrs Campbell, who then toddles off back to her own flat.

As I sit on the edge of the bed with my legs dangling over the edge, still a good two feet off the ground may I add, it strikes me that Mrs Campbell only ever wears slippers, I have never seen her in a pair of shoes, not even when its raining or snowing, and she also wears this blue bib style apron which would probably stand up itself if she took it off, all of which is very surprising as all she does all day is clean and hang out washing round the back court.

Sitting there gazing out into this tiny flat I never realised just how small it is, apart from the recess bed we have a pull down couch against one wall, this pulls down into a bed for my parents to use, we also have a big black and grey looking fire and hearth on the wall facing the recess which would have been used for cooking in the past, but we have a small two ring gas hob which stands right next to the sink, the sink is located right in front of the window on the same wall as the fire and this is where we wash clothes, dishes and ourselves,at this point I have to say I don't think its right a lad of 11 years old should be standing in a sink for the world to see on a Sunday night getting washed for school, when the only window in the flat is opened half way with the only thing saving your blushes is a net curtain.

Next to the gas hob we have a stand up cupboard / larder where all the food is stored, this has two frosted glass doors at the top for dishes, the middle section pulls down to provide a worktop,and the two bottom doors open to reveal pots / pans and tins of food, then we have a tallboy on the same wall, this is a chest of drawers which stores all the family's clothes, on top of which sits our small television, which is only ever switched on for the Kathy Kirby show, and that's it, our whole family and belongings squashed into a space twelve feet by twelve feet.

Toffs in the Tenement

"Rupert, RUPERT! Get a grip, eh! I mean snap out of it!" Mother shouts, remembering just in time to correct her speech. " I need you to go the shop and pick up some groceries your Father will be home soon and I need to prepare his tea", Mother had never visited Walters, our local shop, I am sure she thinks the Brigton Derry is a shop that sells cheese and milk , the reason everyone uses Walters is he lets you shop and pay at the end of the week on payday, Mother informs everyone "We have an account at Walters", She doesn't realise that the whole street has an account at Walters.

Walking down the stairs with my small list of groceries in my hand which contains such items as, small tin of beans, one tomato and two eggs , I meet Mr Bain (no first name again) coming up the stairs . "Awright", he grunts, "Hello", I reply. Mr Bain is a scary man who works as a coalman and is always covered from head to toe in dirt. He wears a donkey jacket over his dirty clothes and always smells of whisky. He has had the same rolled up cigarette dangling from the corner of his mouth ever since I've known him, he stays in the top flat with his wife, "Am bursting furra pish", he declares. "Smashing", Is all I could think to say back to him, well what can you say? "Yes you do look as if you are definitely bursting for a pish and I fully sympathise with your plight", I wish I had said that, just see what he would have done.

I leave the dark of the close, and enter the street, my eyes have hardly acclimatised to the sun when I hear this voice shout "Awright son dae ye want a chip!", old Mr McKay hadn't managed to make his way home yet and was quite happily waving his now empty whisky bottle in the air saying cheers to anyone who walked by, I really hoped the liquid flowing into the road from the pavement from underneath him was spilled whisky.

I run up the street and turn the corner at The Dog Leg pub and reach Walters which is in wee Heron St, there are two people in front of me so I am left standing at the entrance of the shop that is how small the shop is. I can hear Walter saying to some lad "Look am no taking they ginger boattles ye never bought them here", The boy leaves the shop muttering "Ah'll take them tae Beatrices then". Beatrice's was a shop at the other end of Heron St on Dalmarnock Rd. " Next", Walter shouts, "Kin ye geez the money fur these Embassy coupons Walter?", asks Mr Mills "How many?", Walter asks, "A hunner", comes the reply. Walter duly counts the coupons and hands over the 3/~6d, "How much dae ah owe ye this week?", asks Mr Mills, "3/~9d",comes the reply from Walter. "There ye go then, kin ah owe ye the thruppence?" asks Mr Mills as he hands back the 3/~6d for the Embassy coupons. "That's fine", says Walter. Mr Mills leave the shop a happy man, safe in the knowledge his debt to Walter has been reduced to Thruppence without any money changing hands.

"Next ", says Walter, "Ah young Rupert, how ur you the day?" asks Walter, "I'm fine thanks", I say as I hand over my list. Walter lines up the items from the list on his cramped counter, he adds up the total cost, scribbles on my list and hands it back. "Gie that tae yer Maw and tell her Mondays fine", he says. I gather up my groceries and am just about to leave when Walter says, "Haud oan Rupert, av goat a joke fur ye", he says sniggering at the same time, "Whit kind a fish sleeps at the bottom o' ra sea?", he asks trying not to laugh, "I don't know", I say, "A kipper", he announces while howling with laughter at the same time. "That's pish", says this small boy about 7 years old, who had wondered in unnoticed. Standing there with half his index finger shoved up his right nostril and the other hand plunged deep into his short trousers pocket. His red hair was standing bolt upright with a flat section at the side were he must have been lying down , he also had a dirty face with bright red cheeks and the remains of a strawberry ice pole clearly visible on his lips. "That wiz in ra Dandy last week", he continues "Gonnae sell me a loosy I'm in a hurry", he demands. The fact that a loosy is a single cigarette, and the boy was about 7 years old provokes a response from Walter of "Bugger off ya wee shite afore a tell yer Maw oan ye", on that note I say cheerio to Walter and head home with the groceries.

On arrival at château Nairn mother has been busy setting the table for tea. She insisted on setting the table every night even though we had virtually nothing to put on it. The table itself was one of those tables that had two flaps you had to lift up; we only had one flap up as there wasn't any room for two. None of the dishes matched and we only had four forks, two knives and two mugs. "Tea will be ready in about twenty minutes", Mother announces, just then the front door opens and in walks Father, "Good evening everyone", he says sounding rather pleased with himself ,while hanging his jacket up on a hook behind the front door "How are we all ?, on this lovely evening", he asks cheerily.

"What has he got to be so bloody happy about?" Wilhelmina mutters under her breath while reading a six month old edition of the Bunty. She receives a glare from mother which basically means I heard you saying bloody. "Tea will be ready in twenty minutes", Mother says, without even turning round from the sink, for some reason she was trying to pretend she hasn't noticed Fathers good mood. "Great news", Father declares, "What", Wilhelmina and me shout excitedly in unison, "What", we shout again, "Well", says father, "There is a chance I might get my old job back", he enthuses. This statement is met with a prolonged sigh from Wilhelmina and me, and absolutely no response from Mother. The reason for this underwhelming response is simple, at least once every month for the last two years we have heard this proclamation. It is usually followed by "No this time its different", or " This time its definitely different", personally speaking I would have been happy with "We are all going to the carnival over the Glasgow green tonight", or "We are all going to the Continental café for a fish tea", Father continues "No this time its different" (I told you) "I met one of my old colleagues who told me my old boss has retired now, and the new boss is looking to recruit a bank manager for Anniesland Cross branch, Isn't that great news?", "great", mumbles Wilhelmina, "Smashing", I say with false enthusiasm, "Super news , now sit down at the table your tea is ready", Mother snaps, this usually means that subject of conversation is finished.

As I said, this scenario only happens every once and while, then father will carry on as normal, what Mother doesn't know is, that I know what embezzlement means now, and there is as much chance of Father getting a job in a bank, as Mother going to the steamie with a bagwash.

Talking of the steamie or wash house as Mother calls it, I had the misfortune of being volunteered (by my Mother) to help Mrs Campbell with two prams worth of dirty washing. For some strange reason there is an abundance of old prams in Brigton, they are used for going to the steamie with your dirty washing, they are also used for bogies or guidies, these are old prams used by children for racing each other and consist of a prams wheels, a plank of wood, and a rope tied to the front wheels for steering. You are then pushed down a hill and left to your own devices, as brakes are never a priority I have seen quite a few bloodied and scraped knees, when this fact is realised and the inevitable crash arises, Oh! And on the odd occasion prams are used for pushing babies around in.

It turns out one of the prams full of washing is ours and Mother pays Mrs Campbell 2/~6d, to do the washing for her, so the plan was I follow Mrs Campbell pushing this pram full of washing to the steamie. When we arrive the first thing to hit you is the smell, the smell of dirty washing, clean washing and wet washing mixed with soap and bleach. There is steam everywhere with people appearing and disappearing like ghosts walking through it, as we venture further inside we are greeted by the sight of loads of women in various shapes, sizes and age hanging over sinks with washboards, they are all wearing scarves of some sort, some have rollers in their hair with a scarf on back to front, some have scarves fully covering their hair. I think a few of them should have covered their faces as well, the sight of all these women from the back jiggling from side to side using their washboards reminded me of the elephants marching in the cartoon the jungle book, then the chief elephant approached, this enormous woman, with a growth of hair on her face that my Father would have been proud off, she informs Mrs Campbell "Thurz a sink owr rer naebdae's yoozing", so we push the washing along the line to the spare sink, I should say two sinks, there is a big sink and a small sink with this big roller with a handle in the middle of them.

On the way past I heard the strangest excerpts of conversations like "Aye she keeps a clean hoose that yin", and "Cause ah don't huv nuffin, disnae mean ah need tae huv durty claes", my personal favourite being "See me, see ma man we alwiz dae rat." It was like there own language of steamie talk. I was about to leave after parking the pram at the allotted sink when I hear "Haw baw heid wer j fink yoor gon, ah need ye tae turn ra mangle", (Rollers)That was me, stuck, for four hours with Mrs Campbell and a herd of scary Glasgow washerwoman....

Anyway, back to us having our tea and Fathers great news, after we have finished eating I ask for permission to go out and play, "Where are you going?" asks Father, "I will probably join my friends down the Booly", I answer. Mother stops what she is doing, "The Booly", she exclaims in a loud voice, "It's far too dangerous to play down there", she continues, "Just play in the street at the front were I can see you", she insists. The reason for this concern is that the Booly has a mysterious past. The Booly is a large piece of waste ground behind the back courts of Heron St, separated by the wall of the back courts. It runs the full length of the street and stretches about 200 yards outwards towards London Rd. It has three disused train tunnels running under London Rd and Dalmarnock Rd. Every gangster, hoodlum and serial killer has been spotted in the Booly at some time, there was even a rumour that Adolph Hitler was hiding in the Dalmarnock Rd tunnel.

It is also a place were gangs meet to settle their differences The Brigton Derry, the Spur, the Tongs, there is even a gang called the Dickie, you have the "Big tongs" for the older guys and the "Wee tongs" for the younger guys, but the Dickie is just called the Dickie for some reason, but all this happens after 9pm and the Booly is left to the children during the day and early evening. But to save any trouble I agreed to play at the front. "You'll be wanting your pocket money then", says Father. Wilhelmina decides to join the conversation at this point, "Yes please Father", Wilhelmina gushes. He reaches into his pocket and brings out two single shillings, he passes one to me and one to Wilhelmina, we both say "Thank you", at the same time, and rush for the front door.

Toffs in the Tenement

Wilhelmina and I stand at the close entrance excitedly trying to decide how to spend our new found wealth, the sun has gone but it is still quite light. Wilhelmina declares "I'm keeping mine for the pictures tomorrow", "What are you going to do with your money?",She asks, This was a good question as I had loads of different options, I could blow it all on penny trays in Beatrice's or keep it for the minors on Saturday, The minors is the pictures for young people on a Saturday morning, were we can watch Zorro and Flash Gordon etc and follow the story every week, I had enough for the entrance fee and a jubilee, a jubilee is orange juice in a small carton which is frozen, and, they take ages to finish. But I had made my mind up, Beatrice's wins, my favourite comic The Sparky 6d, an MB bar 2d and four penny trays.

The minors is rubbish anyway I convince myself, when I left the minors last week the walls with big spikes sticking out of them were closing in on Zorro, one spike was nearly poking out his eye, if I went back tomorrow he should be a human pin cushion, but I bet you any money the walls will be about Ten feet away again and he will get rescued anyway, definitely Beatrice's I reaffirm to myself.

Wilhelmina meets her working class posh friend Leticia, who stays in a 2 bedroom flat in Bernard St, and off they go toward Bernard St each complimenting the other on their choice of hair bands, I head in the opposite direction towards Beatrice's, mulling over the possibility of having two MB bars and two penny trays

As I reach the last close in Heron St, Mrs McKay is still at her window, I glance down her close and see Mr McKay sitting outside his front door, banging the back of his head off the door shouting "C'mon wummin let me in, ah've goat chips", I look at Mrs McKay slightly confused and she says "Ah'll let him stew fur a wee while yet son, then ah'll let him in", I smile politely and keep walking, I cross the road at the corner of Heron St and Dalmarnock Rd and go into Beatrice's, "This is a great shop" I think to myself, there were sweets everywhere, there must have been about 10 children in front of me including my friend Sammy Graham, Sammy is the same age as me but we attend different schools, he is interested in just about everything I am, except he is a brilliant football player, and I am just okay, he stays two closes up from me at 47 Heron St in a room and kitchen, his dad works in a big engineering place in Dunn St called Arrols.

Sammy is the only other person I know apart from me who wants to go to university. "Rupert", he shouts beckoning me to near the front of the queue, everybody else turns round to face me and the usual chorus of Rupert, Rupert in mock posh voices echoes round the shop. It only stops when Beatrice shouts "Enough of that now". Beatrice is a big woman but short, you can hardly see her behind the counter, but there was silence immediately, no-one could take the chance of being barred from this shop, plus she had a big Alsatian. The queue dwindled quickly as everybody got their sweeties and marched out the shop smiling, next it was Sammy and me, "The Sparky please, two MB bars and two penny trays", I say, Beatrice obliges quickly and efficiently, "The same for me except I want the Beezer", Sammy chips in, both of us choose our sweets from the tray, and lift our comics off the counter and hand over our shillings, "Thank you", both of us say at the same time as we turn around and leave the shop.

Outside the shop we fold the comics and put them in our back pockets, we stash the loose sweets in our front pockets and make a start on the MB bars as we cross the road and head back up Heron St. "Dae you want tae play bools?", asks Sammy, his mouth smothered in chocolate, "My marbles are in the house", I reply, "If I go up the stair to get them I'll get kept in",I continue. So we decide just to sit at the close at eat our sweets.

As we walk back up Heron St ,the street is packed with adults and children, there are groups of girls dotted the length and breadth of the street playing ropes, elastics,peaver and Baws (Balls), the latter involves bouncing two balls of the wall and catching them again, while singing a rhyme, There are a group of boys picking teams in readiness to start a game of football halfway up the street, otherwise known as a 'sidey', looking at the amount of boys standing with their hands in the air shouting "Pick me, Pick me", it could end up 17 a side, parents are hanging out the open windows chatting to each other or just listening to the different songs being sung by the girls below, and singing along with them. Some were just watching the hustle and bustle going on below them, their heads moving from side to side like the pigeons in George square, up and down the length of the street trying not to miss anything. We settle down with our sweets and comics, sitting just to the side of my close with our backs against the wall and blend in to this busy street scene.

Darkness starts to fall and the first dreaded cry is heard, This is a cry that strikes fear into every child that hears it, "Jimmy, Sadie, time tae cum up the stair", They both let out a prolonged cry of "Aw Naw", at the same time, and, from different ends of the street, the other kids now know its just a matter of time before its their turn. The football match is finely balanced at 57 each, girls have been waiting ages for their shot of jumping the ropes instead of cawing, but everyone can sense its going to be them shouted next.Sally, John, Jeanie, Marjorie, Kenny, Steven one by one the street empties, "Sammy" ,comes the call from his mum, we say our goodbyes, he heads home, and I head up the close. Wilhelmina and I have an arrangement with our parents, to avoid a ribbing from everybody in the street, they don't shout our names from the window, and we come home when Sammy is shouted up the stair. With the lights from all the flats windows illuminating the street, I head up the close. The close looks different at night, it's like going through that first door of the ghost train at the carnival, its dark, dingy and you don't know what's around the dimly lit corners. The one light at the entrance of the close is extremely dull; I think the bulb is on its last legs, I could generate more light myself with a good idea. Walking up the uneven stairs I can hear every cough from every house, Mr and Mrs Campbell are having an argument about who last made the tea, and Mr Bains' television is turned up that loud I can hear the theme tune of Till death us do part.

I am just about to open my front door when Wilhelmina arrives, she is totally out of breath after taken the stairs two at a time, and is huffing and puffing like the big bad wolf, she eventually nods at me to indicate I can now open the door, and the both of us enter the house.

Once inside Wilhelmina heads straight for the sink to get washed, as I swing behind the door and grab the key to the toilet from the hook "I'm off to the toilet", I shout to nobody in particular, "The- cloak-room", Mother says like a school teacher, "I'm off to the cloakroom", I repeat feeling slightly silly. Going to the outside toilet at night in a tenement isn't quite as simple as its sounds, it can be very scary walking down that one flight of stairs in the semi darkness, once you reach the toilet and put that key in the door and turn it ,you imagine you can hear all sorts of living things scatter, as you open the door, the only light available is from the moon shining through a small window way above your head, there wasn't any electricity in our toilet, there wasn't any glass in the window and the door had a 6 inch gap at the bottom, it was absolutely freezing. The toilet chain was gone and been replaced with string which I could just about reach, and a 2 day old newspaper was torn into strips and stuck on a nail behind the door, thankfully I wouldn't be needing that at this time.

On returning to the flat I am reminded by mother to wash my hands and get ready for bed, for a 11 year old boy this was getting more difficult to do as Wilhelmina had already closed the curtains in the bed recess to get ready for bed herself, I had to undress at the front door next to the coal bunker, just out of sight of Mother and Father who were sitting on the couch.

Soon I have my pyjamas on and I head over to the larder were mother is standing, she checks I haven't scrimped on the wash process by pulling my ears back, looking at my neck, back and front, she then pulls my bottom lip down with her thumb to check my teeth, the whole process is similar to that of a farmer buying a prize bull. Once I have passed inspection, she hands me a small cup of milk, and a slice of bread and butter with sugar sprinkled on it. As Wilhelmina joins me on the couch next to father, he puts down his paper takes off his glasses and turns to face us, "Who would like to go to the carnival tomorrow", he asks, slightly bracing himself for the expected response, with a mouthful of bread in my mouth my response sounds like "Mmmmmm", instead of "Me", Wilhelmina doesn't hold back and sprays me and Father with half eaten bread in her eagerness to confirm she would love to go to the carnival. As father lets us know the details of our planned trip he finishes by saying "Right you two time for bed", after saying goodnight to Mother and Father Wilhelmina climbs into bed first, followed by me, once we are in Father closes the recess curtains, the curtains now become a wall, and we are not allowed outside them until morning. I can hear Father pulling down the couch bed as I go through the nightly ritual with Wilhelmina of "Your leg touched mine", "You touched me first", before long she is flat against the wall and I am on the outside edge of the bed, facing a possible 4 foot drop may I add, with enough room between us for the Harlem Globetrotters basket ball team.

When father turns out the lights there is an eerie silence, the only light in the flat is coming from the street light outside which is quite close to our window, the light penetrates through gaps in the recess curtains to cast weird shadows in our little bed space. I fall asleep looking forward to the carnival the next day, and wondering if Mr McKay ever got into his house.

Toffs in the Tenement

Ra' Shows Ur 'or ra' Green

When I open my eyes the daylight shines through the gaps in the curtains illuminating the bed recess where me and my sister Wilhelmina are sleeping, as my eyes adjust to the light I can hear the ascending high pitch whistle of a kettle boiling and the chink of cups and plates, I notice my sister has moved her original sleeping position and is now lying across the bed with her feet pushing the curtains away from the bed. I reach for the middle of the curtains but they are opened wide by Father followed by the usual "Are you both going to sleep all day?" ,Wilhelmina grunts some inaudible objections before pulling a blanket over her head, as I gingerly slide out of the bed and onto the cold linoleum covered floor.

"Good morning Rupert", Mother says, "Good morning Mother, Father", I respond, he is totally oblivious to my response as he is twiddling knobs on our old radio trying to find a signal, the dulcet tones of Georgie Fame singing Bonnie and Clyde seems to meet his requirements and he continues across the room towards the front door, he puts on his jacket and announces "I'm away to buy a paper". I slowly make my way towards the sink, still coming to terms with the day, when Mother asks "Would you like some toast?", as she puts two slice of bread on the front grill of a small two bar electric fire, I nod to indicate yes, and on reaching the sink turn on the only tap as I look out the window, at least its not raining I think to myself ,the water is freezing cold, as I daintily splash some on my face, I quickly dry off what little water I have on my face, as Mother is distracted by the toast, I'm hopeful she wont notice and make me repeat the process.

Down below our Window I can hear Father speaking to Mr Graham (my friend Sammy's dad) but can't make out what they are saying, they are probably talking about football or the weather I presume. Then a couple of minutes later as I am putting on my clothes near the front door, I can hear Mrs Campbell talking to Mrs Bain out on the landing, I can only make out a couple of words 'Shows' and 'Bingo' and that's when I realize its Saturday and Father is taking us to the carnival today.

The morning tiredness suddenly leaves me to be replaced with anticipation and excitement, "Wilhelmina", I shout, as I pull back one curtain of the bed recess, Wilhelmina sits bolt upright still half asleep and mumbles "Please, don't make me caw again", at this point I wish I had a camera, her usually well groomed blond hair is sticking up and out in every direction, a bit like a cartoon character left holding the bomb that explodes, she has one arm in a duffle coat we use on the bed as an extra blanket and the shape of a duffle coat button embedded temporarily on the left side of her bright red face where she has been sleeping on it, "Remember we are going to the carnival today" I say excitedly, Wilhelmina, on seeing my smiling face, has slipped back into big sister mode by this point, and as she jumps down from the bed she sticks her nose in the air and stomps past me heading towards the chair by the fire to pick up her clothes "I know we are going to the carnival", she says matter of factly, on her return to the bed recess she jumps up and kneels on the edge of the bed facing me, she grabs a curtain in each hand and looks me straight in the eye , and sticks her tongue out in my direction, before quickly closing the curtains.

Just then Father returns with his paper, everybody else's Father reads the Daily Record, mines' buys the Herald, which lasts a lot longer than the Record as toilet paper it has to be said, he makes his way to the couch to read his paper just before the bed recess curtains swing open and Wilhelmina makes her entrance, she gets dressed quicker than Clark Kent in a phone box I thought to myself.

Her hair is brushed and pinned with a red hair band holding it together that matches her red dress, her red shoes at the side of the couch complete her ensemble, and she now officially looks like one of the Brady Bunch. "Breakfasts ready", Mother announces, Mother has set the table again with the exact same dishes as we used for our dinner the night before, she puts a slice of buttered toast on each plate, followed by a glass of milk, the smell of the buttered toast is making me even more hungry than I already am, but we are not allowed to eat until everyone is seated at the table, and Father is sitting on the couch engrossed in some item in his newspaper, "Ahem", is all it takes from Mother, to have him jumping up, as if the couch had just caught fire,, and join us at the table.

"Wire in" er! "Tuck in everyone", Mother says correcting her self quickly, as we are eating Father announces that he has to go into work to pick up his pay, Mother then also announces that she and Wilhelmina are going to the west end to visit friends and do a bit of window shopping, "What about me, what about the carnival ?", I ask "You'll just have to stay here until we all return, we can go to the carnival another day", says Father, great I thought, stuck inside all day and no carnival.

"Right I'm off", he says, rising off his chair with a half slice of toast sticking out his mouth, he puts on his jacket and leaves. A couple of minutes later there is a knock at the front door, "Can you answer the door Rupert?" Mother asks, I slowly make my way to the door, nearly stepping on my petted lip, and as I open it my mood changes immediately, its my friend Sammy, he is looking very shiny and new, his wet hair has a perfect side parting, brand new multi coloured striped t-shirt, and new denims with a six inch turn-up, he sees me staring and says "I know, I know ma maw goat a Provvie cheque", "I goat these tae", he says lifting up the bottom of his denims to reveal a new pair of sandshoes, sandshoes or sannies as they are known around here, are a pair of cloth shoes with a rubber sole and a black rubber toecap.

"Ur ye coming tae the minors?", asks Sammy, "I can't", I reply "I have to stay in the house today", I continue, "But your da, told ma da this morning it would be okay fur ye tae go", says Sammy with a puzzled expression on his face, just then I heard a familiar "Ahem", I turn round to see Mother standing there with a shilling in her hand, and a smile on her face, "Your Father was only kidding you this morning", she says " He told Mr Graham this morning it would be okay for you to go to the minors with Sammy, and ,when you both come back we are all going to the carnival", she declares.

My face lights up again, I invite Sammy in as I have to put my shoes on, and we head over to the couch with big smiles on our faces. "What about the west end?", Wilhelmina asks completely aghast at what she has just witnessed, "We can go tomorrow" answers mother "You can help me tidy up today and get some messages er! groceries", she says correcting herself once again. With my shoes now on, I motion with my head to Sammy letting him know its time to go, as we make our way across the room towards the front door, Mother is standing at the sink with her back to us, "Where do you think your going?", she asks without even looking round, Sammy looks at me sympathetically as we know what is about to happen, "Come here till I have a look at you", she orders, I slowly troop over to the sink, where mother is already in the process of licking her thumb, she proceeds to rub her thumb up and down each side of my cheeks while manoeuvring my hair with her other hand, this is known to every child in Brigton as a 'Mammy wash' ,after drying my face with my sleeve I say goodbye to her, turn round and stick my tongue out at Wilhelmina, who is sitting there with a big grin on her face, and head out with Sammy to the minors.

We head down the stairs, discussing whether Zorro will become a human pincushion when the walls with the spikes close in on him , just as we are near the entrance of the close when hear a frail voice shouting "Haw yoos two, haud oan a minute" we turn around to find Old Mrs McLean shuffling towards us. Mrs McLean lives in the ground floor flat and must be the oldest woman in Brigton, her two tone grey hair is held in place with about ten kirbies, her face is wrinkled with lots of straggly grey facial hair, her chest sinks southward past her waist and over her apron pointing towards her feet, where her socks have fallen around her ankles, she shuffles further towards us in her furry slippers with the heels squashed flat, and asks "Kin ye go tae Walters fur me, and get me a wee loaf and a block 'o good butter?", before we can say anything, she puts a two bob bit in my hand and starts to shuffle back to her house.

Left with no option we decide to run round to Walters as fast as we can, as we don't want to be late for the minors, when we arrive at Walters we jump in the shop, both of us shouting "I won", Huffing and puffing we stand at the counter trying to catch our breath, Walter asks "Whit can get you lads this mornin", "A wee loaf... and. a ..block... of good butter", I say between breaths, "Old Mrs Mc Lean?", Walter asks , I am too out of breath to say anything, so just nod in agreement with my hands on my knees. "Aye she owes me hauf a croon that wummin, and hisnae been in here fur about three weeks, the auld bugger", he continues," I'll let her know", I say, with no intention of doing anything. We pay for the loaf and butter and head back to Mrs McLean as fast as we can.

We chap her door and wait, and wait, and wait "The auld bugger's gonny make us late for the minors", an agitated Sammy moans, "Watch yer lip ya wee shite",old Mrs McLean snipes, as she approaches us from behind "A wiz hinging oot a washing in the back", we hand over her loaf and butter along with her change, she puts the change in a pocket in her apron, then offers me a ha'penny to split with Sammy. "Thanks fur nothing", mumbles Sammy, "Whit wiz that?", Mrs McLean says abruptly, "Is that fur muffins?", Sammy says a little bit louder pointing at the butter, "Aye" she says, knowing fine well that's not what he said.

We run off as fast as we can down Heron St, saying hello to Mrs McKay who is still hanging out her window as we pass, and turn right onto Dalmarnock Rd, and head for the Bridgeton Toll, when we reach the Cactus Pub we turn right again and can now see the queue for the minors outside the Olympia picture house stretching back towards the Salvation army.

The Toll is a hive of activity at this time of day, buses travelling in all directions, London rd, Dalmarnock Rd, Main St and James St, you can hear a repetitive thump, thump as the buses cross the old tram lines, the smell of the exhaust fumes is thick in the air, and there are vans outside shops busily being loaded and unloaded, a man stands in the Toll selling newspapers shouting in what seems like a foreign language at the top of his voice, stopping every now and again to take swig out of a bottle of beer. I also notice a policeman standing outside his call box having a cigarette as we cross the weighbridge and join the end of the queue.

A couple of minutes after joining the queue I hear a voice shouting hello Roooopirt , I look ahead and see Jamie and John Mc Cabe, luckily for me the queue starts to move and the McCabe twins are pushed in the direction of the entrance by the people behind them, saving me any embarrassment and quips about being posh ,when we are nearly at the entrance the queue stops temporarily, we are right beside the poster showing the film that's 'coming soon', there are also six photographic stills, the film is called The Sound Of Music and doesn't look very good, There's a photo of a lady standing on a hill, another of a group of children that look as if they are singing , hardly in the same league as James Bond ,Sammy and I agree that it wont be very successful.

As the queue starts to move again there is a feeling of excitement and anticipation as we approach the kiosk, "next", the woman in the kiosk shouts, "One please", I say , followed by Sammy, the woman in the kiosk just sits there smoking a cigarette and slides the tickets over to the opening in the glass front of the kiosk, "Hurry up and move yer arse" she says as we struggle to lift our tickets, after paying our entrance fee we buy a jubilee from an usherette, I would love one of those big ice-cream tubs or a Fab ice lolly that she has in her tray which hangs round her neck, but they cost the equivalent of about five trips to the minors " That'll be a thruppence ", she says as she hands me my jubilee "Thank you very much", I say as I hand over my money, "Don't be a smart arse", She replies "Now move", she continues , Sammy has always quite fancied her and cheekily asks "Any chance a' a kiss", "Ye'll get ma toe up yer arse if a get ony mer a' yer cheek", is her instant reply, "Aye awright", Sammy says "Geeza jubilee then", I don't know what he saw in her anyway, she was ancient, she must have been about eighteen .

Anyway as we make our way to our seats, as usual, there is absolute bedlam in the hall kids everywhere shouting at each other, standing on the seats, throwing empty cartons about the place, the poor usherettes have long giving up trying to keep order. The manager comes on to the stage with a microphone and appeals to no avail for everyone to calm down, eventually he gives up and leaves the stage, then the magic happens, the lights go down, the curtains open and the music starts, everyone sits down immediately and after a minute of applause and cheering there is total silence as the film begins.

A couple of hours later the doors of the Olympia fly open and around a hundred excited kids leave the minors, fencing with each other with invisible swords, me and Sammy included, as we make our way home heading down Dalmarnock Rd towards Heron st, we are talking about how Zorro will escape the quicksand next week, when I hear my fathers voice, "Rupert", he shouts as he comes out of Woolworths, "Hello Father", I say as I turn around, "Awright Mr Nairn?" Sammy asks "Yes I'm fine Sammy thanks for asking", he replies not realising it wasn't a rhetorical question but a statement, "Are you Awright yoursel? ,he asks Sammy with a contented look on his face, trying to sound like a local, but still sounding like a BBC newsreader, Sammy just nods and takes a couple of steps back with his hands in his pockets, "Did you enjoy the minors then lads?" he asks, "Great", I say nodding "Aye great", Sammy adds shuffling about with his shoulders up at his ears, its amazing how kids can talk among themselves like budgies for hours on end, but as soon as an adult arrives you cant get a word out them, "Well I've got a couple of errands to run, you two go straight home we've got the carnival to go to",he says as he crosses the road and disappears into Lennox's.

When me and Sammy approach Heron St a large crowd of men and woman come round the corner, they are all dressed very smartly in their suits and dresses, the lady in the middle of the crowd is carrying a baby in a white shawl, they are all laughing and joking as they pass either side of Sammy and me, and as they pass we are nearly knocked out by the smell of strong perfumes and aftershaves. A fat man at the back of the crowd stops right beside me, he ruffles my hair with his fat fingers, and says "Here ye go son" and hands me this small parcel of tin foil, "Shift yer fat arse Archie", one of the other men shouts "Yoor buying ra furst round", he continues laughing out loud, the fat man then breaks into a half jog to catch up with the rest of the group.

I open the tinfoil and inside are two Abernethy biscuits with butter in the middle, as I look at Sammy with a confused look on my face, he is eying up the biscuits jealously, "One for you" I say to Sammy as I split the biscuits and hand one to him, "And one for me", when I look at the one I have, to my astonishment there is two sixpences in the butter, Sammy looks at his biscuit when he sees what is in mine, "Nothing" he declares with a petted lip, turning his biscuit upside down, as we walk round the corner into Heron St, I pick one sixpence out of the butter on my biscuit and hand it to a delighted Sammy "Thanks" he says gratefully as he unwittingly wipes the butter off the sixpence on his new T-shirt, I pick out the other one and clean it with the tin foil and put it in my pocket, "That'll do for the carnival " I say to Sammy, we then break up the biscuits and feed them to some hungry pigeons who have been taking a keen interest in our activities ever since we opened the tinfoil.

When we reach my close I say goodbye to Sammy and arrange to meet him at the carnival later. I run up the stairs and stop at the landing where the outside toilet is, the landing window is open and I can see two lads about 8 years old, one of them is up on top of the brick shed where the large bins are kept, and the other is on the ground standing in the back court. "Jump ya scaredy cat" the one on the ground shouts, "Aye! So a bloody wull", the one on the top replies, "Well jist dreepie it then" the one on the ground shouts "Ah want tae go tae ra lucky middens behind ra shoaps", he continues.

Just then Mrs Campbell my next door neighbour arrives at the entrance of the back court, she spots the boy on the roof and yells, "Haw spiderman, whit ur ye daen up there, get doon afore ah tell yer maw oan ye", "Bugger off ya auld fart" comes the reply from spiderman, "Aye bugger off", his friend on the ground agrees, "Right that's it ya cheeky wee bastards I'll get ma man tae yiz, JOHN", she shouts up the close, "JOHN" she shouts again, before John can make an appearance ,the boy on the roof jumps onto the wall that separates the backcourt from the Booly, his pal on the ground climbs up to join him on top of the same wall, they then turn and mimic Mrs Campbell's cries for help "JOHN, JOHN" and then run along the wall towards Dalmarnock Rd, shouting obscenities at poor Mrs Campbell .

"If ah get ma hauns oan they wee bastards ah'll string them up so ah wull", she grumbles as she heads back in the close, "JOHN were ur ye ya lazy bastard", she shouts again as she starts to walk up the stairs, just then

Toffs in the Tenement

I hear the toilet next to me flush, and Mr Campbell opens the toilet door still pulling up his braces, and asks "Whit ur ye shouting at wummin, I wiz daen a shite?", "Ach yer always daen a shite"she growls "Yer too late noo ya lazy good fur nothing lump a' widd ", She replies," two lads wur geen me cheek", she adds "Nae wunner" Mr Campbell whispers sarcastically as he quickly heads up to his house, "Ah'll nae bloody wunner ye when a get up they stairs , ya useless pile a shite", Mrs Campbell rants as she follows him up the stairs as fast as she can.

Even though I have become used to hearing Mrs Campbell's fruity language it can still be quite scary when she is in full flow, so I wait on the landing till she enters her house, still ranting and raving at Mr Campbell, before making my way up the stairs to my house.

"Hello mother" I say as I enter the house, "Hello Rupert" she replies as she stuffs sandwiches into her string bag, she is packing our lunch for the carnival, "Where's Wilhelmina", I ask, "Oh she went to the swimming baths with her friend Leticia" she replies, while standing with a rain mate in one hand and sun cream in the other, "Only in Glasgow", she exclaims, shaking her head and shoving both in the bag, The sun cream bottle was over 4 years old and empty, it was only ever brought out when there was an opportunity to show off to the neighbours.

"Mother can you dry my hair for me?", Wilhelmina asks, as she comes flying through the front door, and throws her wet towel on the couch, "I'm far too busy" she replies "But look at the state of my hair", Wilhelmina exclaims, its not often I agree with Wilhelmina but she did look a right state, her hair was hanging down covering her face, Which was an improvement, and was soaking wet, and dripping all over the linoleum. "Come over here", she orders, and grabs our other towel and starts rubbing Wilhelmina's head like a madwoman, "Ow, ow, ah, ah, ow, ah, ah, ow, ah owwwww", Wilhelmina cries, I am sitting on the couch enjoying every minute of her suffering.

At that moment, Father returns from his errands, he is carrying two bags, one large and one small, he heads over to the larder and pulls down the middle section, the large bag is full of boring things like potatoes, milk, sausages etc, but the smaller bag has the goodies. As he empties the bag he describes each item one by one as he lays them on the worktop, "Ginger, crisps, biscuits, Ayton sandwich biscuits no less" he boasts, "Quarter of jelly babies for me, and a bar six for Mother", he continues, then he stops "What about us",I say disappointedly, "The bag seams to be empty" he answers, before turning round with two tubes of smarties, panic over.

Toffs in the Tenement

Wilhelmina heads for the bed recess to get changed and I get asked to stand outside in the landing until Mother gets changed, when I am invited back in, she is standing in front of the small mirror we have hanging above the chest of drawers, fixing her hair. She looks lovely in her green dress and matching hat, Wilhelmina exits the bed recess back to her Brady bunch best and Father is standing there with three full bags of stuff we are taking with us to the carnival "Right everyone ready , lets go", he announces.

I run down the stairs taking them two at a time, and I'm at the entrance of our the close before Father has locked the door of our flat, its turned into a lovely sunny day and I am bursting with excitement, but my family don't seem to share my enthusiasm as they take forever to appear at the bottom of the stairs but, eventually they join me and we head off down Heron St.

When we reach the bottom of Heron St, we all wave over to Mrs McKay, "Ur yeez away tae the shows?" she shouts as she waves back, "We ur indeed " Father replies, trying once more to sound as if he was born and bred in Bridgeton.

We turn left onto Dalmarnock Rd and cross the road at the petrol station, as we carry on past the grain store, I am about ten yards in front of the rest of the family, I am willing them with all my might to walk faster, as we turn into Muslin St, I can see the trees of the park in the distance ,I am desperate to start running full out ,but Mother has this psychological magnet that holds me back, eventually we cross over the road at Main St onto Tullis St, by this time I am about thirty yards in front and can hear the music from the carnival, I am standing shuffling from one leg to the other as if I need the toilet, while I wait on the rest of the family to catch up, after what feels like an eternity, we cross Greenhead St and reach the lane which takes you right into the carnival, I can now hear the music clearly, see the big wheel and the dive-bomber's and can faintly smell the hot dogs.

With no more roads to cross I'm off like a whippet, my parents shout something, but I haven't got a clue what it is. The lane is only about a hundred yards long but seems to last forever, but I know I am getting nearer as the smell of the food is growing stronger and the noise louder, I glance behind me and see Wilhelmina and my parents way behind, Wilhelmina is about five yards in front of Mother and Father walking fast, but trying hard not to break into a run, although she is just as desperate as me to have a go on the rides. I arrive at the end of the lane where the carnival starts, and I'm running that fast that when I stop, I slide for about three yards just like they do in the cartoons.

I am standing there taking in the whole atmosphere, the noise, the smells, the colour and the sheer excitement of it all, when Wilhelmina arrives by my side closely followed my Mother, and then Father with all the bags. "Well what are you going on first" asks Father "The ghost train" I shout with my hand up in the air as if I'm in class and know the answer to a question, "The motorbikes" Wilhelmina says, as we can't agree Father volunteers to take Wilhelmina to the motorbikes and Mother comes with me to the ghost train.

I have a go on the ghost train, the small octopus, and the cups and saucers, then it was on to the dodgems, Mother stands at the side each time and watches me, waving like a madwoman, as I leave the dodgems I say to her "Why don't you have a go on something?", "No thank you", she replies, she then pauses for a moment and goes on to say, "I might have a go at the bingo", I find this very surprising, the reason I'm surprised is the fact that we have been coming here for three years now and she has never tried anything, not even hoopla at the stalls. "There's the bingo over there", I point out, as far as I know she has never played bingo, so this should be interesting. The bingo at the carnival is a round stall, with about twenty bingo boards all the way round the outside, there is a stool at every board and in the centre of the stall lots and lots of prizes, if you win, you can pick any prize you like. There is also room in the centre for a person to walk round collecting the money and giving out change. Also, in a small space inside the stall sits the person who shouts out the numbers.

When we arrive at the bingo stall, Mother is looking for a seat when she spots a large woman with about four chins get up to leave, "That boards shite" she exclaims to Mother as she passes, "Oh is it", she replies, not having a clue what she was meant to say, she sits down and looks at the boards with a confused look on her face, needing help, she tries to attract the attention of the girl collecting the money. "Excuse me",she says, the girl is standing less than four feet away and doesn't respond, "Excuse me please", she tries again to no avail, "HAW YOO GONNY GEEZ SUM CHANGE", she belts out, the girl jumps and immediately comes over "Awright, awright keep yer hair oan", the girl says, "Could I please have change for a ten shilling note?" Mother asks politely on regaining her composure, "Ur yoo takin' ra piss" comes the reply "Jist geez ra change hen",Mother demands, before handing over 6d for the next game. Mother composes herself again then turns to me and says "Now Rupert I never want to hear you speaking like that, do you understand?", "Yes Mother" I reply still reeling from her antics, she then proceeds to open up all the small doors that cover the numbers on the boards in readiness for the next game.

The bingo caller explains the rules before shouting "Eyes down and your first number is 4 and 3 43"He carries on shouting out numbers and I can see Mother closing quite a lot of boxes very quickly, a few numbers later and she is only waiting on number 13,"one and three 13 ", announces the caller "HOUSE" she shouts, and a chorus of "Awww" emanates from everyone's lips you would have thought she had pulled a gun and threatened everybody judging by the response , "Jammy bastard" one woman mumbles, "Furst time anaw, jammy bugger", another says, The girl checks Mothers numbers and hands her a token ,meaning she can pick anything she likes from the prizes on show.

As she is looking at prizes Father and Wilhelmina arrive, after telling them of Mothers good fortune we all start to look at the prizes," Look at that beautiful painting of the little girl cuddling the puppy", Wilhelmina suggests, "That's a smashing tool kit", Father offers, "That toy car is cracking", is my input, "Ahhhhh!" Says mother when she spots something among the prizes, "That's perfect" she purrs, as she hands over her token to the girl. Now the painting was quite nice, I loved the toy car, and I could played with the toolkit at a push, but what are you meant to do with a three tier cake stand. "Any body hungry", asks Father still staring at the cake stand, he receives three hands in the air in answer to his question, we all agree its time for lunch, the four of us and the cake stand, head over the bridge and into Richmond Park.

We settle down on a blanket near the duck pond and Mother and Wilhelmina start to lay out all the goodies, Father and I head over to feed the ducks with a small bag of old bread that usually goes to the pigeons and sparrows round our back court.

We notice there are people out in the boats having a great time in the summer sun, with old Mr Lafferty keeping a watchful eye on them. Mr Lafferty is in charge of the boats and tells everybody he used to be a sailor during the war, his stories are legendary, he told father that during the war he was captured by the Germans and they tortured him by putting Jimmy Shand records on and nailing his feet to the floor. Father laughed for ages when he heard that one, but I still don't know who Jimmy Shand is. He also tells the kids that when he started work in the park, on his first day he was with his boss, and trying to impress him, he stood at the edge of the pond and shouted out in a loud, clear voice "Come in number 99 yer time is up" his boss pointed out to him they didn't have a number 99, he then thought "Oh shit", and shouted "66 ur ye in trouble?".

When we return having fed the ducks, Mother and Wilhelmina have started eating, we are invited to start eating by Mother saying "Wire In", er, em, "Tuck in you two", she corrects herself hoping we didn't notice. I head straight for an Ayton sandwich biscuit, these diamond shaped biscuits are brilliant, Father opts for a salad sandwich, as it consists of only lettuce and bread and nothing else, I politely refuse his offer of one, before he returns the tinfoil being used as a plate to the blanket.

As we all sit munching away I think to myself "This is a perfect day", when out of the corner of my eye I notice this beautiful swan leaving the pond about ten yards from where we are, as I turn round to get a better view, this swan opens it wings fully and lifts it head in the air, "What a magnificent sight", I think to myself, then it charges straight at us squawking as loud as it can, half running and half flying, "Look out", I shout as I stand up and run, Father tries to help Mother up off the grass, and her hat goes flying into the distance as she loses a shoe trying to get up quick, the two of them slip on the grass and end up entangled like Mick mc Manus and Jackie Pallo wrestling on the telly, Wilhelmina screeches as she tries to run towards the boat shed where the ice cream van would offer some sort of barrier.

The beast from the deep as I know see it tramples right over our blanket, scattering all Mothers lovely food to the four winds, its attention is firmly focused on me, it chases me for about thirty yards, when I decide to turn sharply in an attempt to lose this vicious animal, and head back towards Father, the beast turns just as sharply , still flapping its wings and squawking heading right for me, just then I see old Mr Lafferty who shouts "Drop the biscuit", "What" I reply as I cant hear him with all the commotion, by this time I now have an audience of all the other families pointing and laughing at my predicament , " Wull ye drop the bloody biscuit" Mr Lafferty screams, as I realise what he is saying I throw the biscuit as far as I can to my left, and keep running towards Father , Thankfully the beast turns and heads towards my biscuit, it quickly eats its prize, then nonchalantly walks back to the pond, past the scene of devastation it has caused, and swims away. We all look at Mr Lafferty looking for an explanation, "He likes Ayton sandwich biscuits" he shrugs matter of factly. We all turn to look at each other, and after a moment off silence, burst out laughing.

Mother and Father start to clean up the mess left by the creature from the black lagoon, as my thoughts turn to meeting my friend Sammy when we return to the carnival, "What time is it", I ask, "Ten to three", Father replies, I decide to help out with the clearing up to speed up the process, as I have arranged to 'Bump' into Sammy at three o clock, next to the amusements at the entrance to the carnival.

As we are crossing the big bridge over the Clyde on our way back to the carnival, I suggest to Father he has a go at the darts stall, "You were very good last year", I say, straightening up and puffing out his chest he agrees "I was, wasn't I", the darts stall just happens to be next to the amusements at the entrance of the park.

When we arrive at the darts stall he hands over his money and is given three darts, the scruffy looking man who is in charge of the stall tells him "Anyfing 'or twenty wan and ye wun a prize" Father adopts a professional stance then throws the first dart, it bounces of the wire on the dartboard flies back out and just misses Mother by inches, "That coonts" growls scruffy man, Mother scowls at father as she gently moves another couple of steps back with Wilhelmina, Father adopts the same stance as last time, he launches the dart at the board " seven" scruffy growls, one more to go, so father takes a step back to compose himself, then adopts the position and throws, the dart flies towards the board and thuds into the number twenty, " Twinty seven" scruffy announces , "Well done " Mother enthuses, he points to a big cuddly toy and says to scruffy "I'll take that please", scruffy grins, leans forward and informs Father that the prize he has chosen is only available if you score one hundred or more, "Boatum shelf", he indicates, as Father looks there is a plastic key ring with a skull on it, or a pencil, "I'll have the pencil please", Father says reluctantly.

At that moment I hear a familiar voice shouting "Rupert, Rupert"; it was my friend Sammy with his mum and dad. Strangers walking past stared at me with sympathetic expressions as they had never heard of or seen anyone called Rupert. " Kin me and Rupert play ra amusements da'", asks Sammy, his dad looks at Father, who then looks at Mother who then says "Go on then" to Sammy and me's delight, "Meet back here in half an hour", Sammy's mum adds, considering neither Sammy or me had a watch this last request could prove quite difficult.

Armed with a shilling each we head into the amusements, we walk up to the change counter and declare "6d of pennies and 6d of ha'pennies please" the scruffy woman behind the glass must have been related to the guy at the darts stall, she never said anything, and seemed annoyed she had to put her cigarette down to deal with our request, with our change in our hand we turn round and look at all the fruit machines, we then do what every kid does at the amusements, we walked round all the machines putting our hand in looking for money somebody might have left, when that proves fruitless, I decide to play the one armed bandit, while Sammy has a go on the grand national, after losing 3d each we opt to spend the rest on candy floss.

When we reach the candy floss stand there is no one there, suddenly scruffy from the darts appears behind the counter, "Whit ye wantin'", he growls, at this point I'm thinking "Was that him in the amusements with a wig on", "Two candy floss", I say "We'll pay fur them separate" Sammy adds, he winds the stick around the machine until there are two big candy flosses he hands one to me and one to Sammy "Tanner each", he barks, we hand over the money and proceed to eat our purchases.

"Whit dae ye want tae dae with ra' 3d we've goat left?" asks Sammy, with what looks like the remains of a pink rabbit hanging out his mouth, "Why don't we go back and play it in the amusements" I reply while trying to pull candy floss out my hair, Sammy nods in agreement and we walk the short distance to a different amusements. This one has more electronic machines and is brighter than the last one, Sammy is standing at a penny machine that pays out two shillings for a jackpot, we decide that is the one for us, I put in a penny and push a button the wheels spin round and stop one at a time bell, bell, cherry, then lights start to flash at the bottom of each symbol, "Whit diz that mean" Sammy asks quizzically, "I don't know", I answer, then a voice says "Yiv goat a haud", as we look down there is a small boy aged about five standing there, his dirty face is only matched with his dirty clothes, "Haud yer bells " he suggests, "Pardon", I ask "Dae ye want me tae show ye?", he continues, "Yes, aye", Sammy and me say at the same time, he pushes in front of us and presses the two buttons that are flashing below the bells, "Ye need tae put mer money in", he orders, Sammy reaches over and puts another penny in the slot, we press the button and the bells don't move , only the reel with the cherry, it stops at a melon, and the lights flash again, we follow his instructions four more times until we have put our last penny in, the reels spin, bell, bell, melon, then a light on the right hand side of the machine starts moving up and down, "What does that mean?", I ask our little financial advisor, "Huv ye goat any money left?" he asks, "No,naw "we answer together, "Then that means yer pumped" he answers laughing at our misfortune.

Just then Wilhelmina arrives "Hello boys, what are you up to?" she asks, swinging her little purse on a string she got out of last weeks Bunty, "We wur playing this machine", Sammy replies, "But we don't have any money left now", I add, Wilhelmina then goes into her purse and pulls out a penny, "I'll have a go then", she says, as she puts the penny in the slot, she presses the button and the reels start to spin, Bell, Bell, and...... Bell, all the lights on the machine flash, as me and Sammy look on in amazement, it then starts to spit out pennies "Yippee", Wilhelmina screams, as she starts to scoop them up, at this point Mother and Father arrive with Sammy's parents, "What's going on?", asks Father, "That lassie jist wun the jackpot", our ex financial advisor says,"Wey nae hauds" he continues, obviously impressed. "Well done Wilhelmina", Father says, as Wilhelmina fills her purse with pennies, she smiles that fake smile big sisters do at me and Sammy and deliberately counts her pennies in front of us with a smug grin on her face, "You can buy the chips on the way home", Father adds jokingly, Wilhelmina doesn't reply in case he is serious.

It was then father uttered those dreaded words, "Time to go home I'm afraid", he says "Ohhhhh nooo!", Sammy and I moan in unison, but our protests fall on deaf ears. We say our goodbyes to Sammy and his parents who are staying on a while, and start to make our way towards the lane. "What a great day", I think to myself, as I play it over in my mind, "Are you coming with me to Aldo's for chips when we get home Rupert?" Father asks, as we cross the road at Greenhead St, I nod to confirm his request, as I am starting to feel tired by this time, I am now lagging behind the group, as Mother shouts "Try and keep up Rupert", which I will hear at least another ten times before we reach Heron St.

"Why does it always take ages to travel to the carnival but only takes minutes to get home?" I ask myself.

Toffs in the Tenement

We're 'o gon o'r ra' Barra's

"Naw yer daen it wrang "Sammy snaps, as he gathers up the stones from the ground for the tenth time, "Right look" he orders... Sammy is trying to teach me a game called five stones, we are sitting on the ground, just inside the entrance to my close, and I am struggling to get to grips with this extremely difficult game, it involves throwing a stone in the air and quickly picking up another stone, (with the same hand), off the ground, in time to catch the stone that's in the air before it hits the ground, then you repeat this process and pick up two, then three and so on... "Right am in big wansy, and your in big twosy, ok", he says, looking for confirmation that I understand, before I can say or do anything, we are interrupted by Father coming out of the close, we have to make a space between us to let him pass.

"What are you two up to then?" he asks, "Wur playin five staines" Sammy replies, Father looks at me for a translation with a puzzled expression on his face, "We are playing a game called five stones" I inform him, "Oh I see," he says, " Did you enjoy the carnival yesterday?" he asks Sammy, "Aye" was Sammy's short response, realising there was no point in prolonging the conversation, he finishes off by saying "Wire in then" still trying to sound like a native of Bridgeton, he then heads off down Heron St.

"Right you two shift yer arses" growls Mrs Campbell, who appears from nowhere, and frightens the living daylights out of me and Sammy,

34

there is a distinct smell of old person as she squeezes past us and starts to walk up the stairs, "Ye shoodnae be playin rer any road" she grumbles under her breath, but just loud enough for us to hear. We never noticed her approaching, or the woman she was talking to, as Father was blocking our view, we are still getting over the shock, when we hear a loud whistle, we both look at each other and shout at the same time "RAGMAN".

Sammy runs to his house and I run up the stair to mine, as I enter the house, mother is folding washing and putting it away in the tallboy, "Mother do you have any rags?" ,I say excitedly, "The ragman's coming" "I don't know" she answers," I would have to check" she adds, Mother sends me back out to play, and tells me to come back in ten minutes while she has a look, she informs me that if there is any rags she will leave them on the landing for me as she was about to have a go at mopping the floor, and doesn't want my mucky footprints all over the linoleum, I would love to have stayed and watched mother's attempt at mopping the floor, as we don't have a mop.

I wait at the entrance to the close then I decide that ten minutes must have passed, I slowly walk up the stairs and as I reach the toilet landing halfway up the stairs , my front door comes into view, I can also hear someone in the toilet, who is having a rough time of it, going by the noises and smells that are escaping through the six inch gap at the bottom of the toilet door, as I get closer to my house, there sitting at the side of my door is a bundle of rags, "Brilliant", I think, as I quickly grab the rags and run down the stairs, remembering to hold my breath on the way past the toilet.

When I leave the close I bump into Sammy who has an equally impressive bundle of rags, the both of us run up Heron St towards Bernard St with big smiles on our faces anticipating the gifts that are coming our way. The ragman has stopped his cart, just opposite the Dog Leg pub and there is already a small group of kids gathered around him, his cart is already quite full of rags but I can clearly see the battered old suitcase that contains the toys.

"Wan it a time, Wan it a time", he shouts, as the eager kids jostle for position, The first wee boy in the queue offers his bundle to the ragman, the ragman unfolds it and holds it up in the air, he then looks at the wee boy and asks "Is this your pyjamas?" the wee boy looks sheepish and nods, the ragman shakes his head, and hands the bundle back to the boy, who is now about to burst into tears, "Here" says the ragman handing the wee boy a balloon, the boys face lights up, it was if he had been given all the chocolate he could eat , instead of a wee red balloon.

Toffs in the Tenement

"Next", shouts the Ragman gruffly, not wishing to appear a soft touch, the next boy hands over a donkey jacket with GOVAN SHIPYARDS on it, "Whaur did ye get ris? " asks the Ragman, "Ah fun it", comes the reply, "Pick a toy ren", the ragman says without further questions, as he quickly puts the donkey jacket at the bottom of the clothes piled on his cart so it cant be seen, meanwhile the wee boy who is next, is in the process of taking off his t-shirt, "Naw, naw", groans the Ragman "Am no takin yer claes" he says , waving his dirty index finger from side to side in front of the boys face, I feel sorry for the boy as he walks away with a look of disappointment on his face while tucking his t-shirt back in his short trousers.

Sammy and me are next, we hand over our rags, the Ragman checks my bundle first and seems particularly impressed with a pair of trousers that has a snake belt in the waistband, he then checks Sammy's bundle and says "Help yersel's tae any toy oot ra case", we don't need a second invitation before we are rummaging about in the suitcase, Sammy takes a toy gun with plastic caps, and I take the bow and arrow set, he also gives both of us a whistle.

We agree to meet up later and play with our new toys, meanwhile, we return to our own houses to show our parents what we got for the rags. When I reach my close, having dispensed with the plastic packaging from the bow and arrow set, I decide to try the whistle inside the close as it always sounds much louder, as I reach the bottom of the stairs, I quickly check there is no-one round the back court, then I place the whistle in my mouth, take a deep breath.... ,just then I hear Mothers voice talking to Mrs Campbell up on our landing, I slowly creep up a few more stairs, so I can hear what they are saying , "Am bloody telling ye Mrs Nairn," Mrs Campbell groans, "Some bastard's stole ma' man's claes", she moans, "Ma' pal wiz takin them tae ra bagwash fur me, ah left them oan the landing tae ah went back in the hoose furra minute, an when ah came oot, they wur off".

The blood drains from my face, when I hear Mrs Campbell, and suddenly I don't want the bow and arrow set anymore, or the whistle, "If ah get ma hons the wee shite that's knocked ma' mans claes I'll kick his arse fae here tae kingdom come", Mrs Campbell rants. By this point I am in a panic, as I head to the entrance of the close, still clutching my ill gotten gains, and wondering how you go about joining the French foreign legion, as I look to my left I see Father turning into Heron St, "How do I explain this?" I ask myself, looking at the bow and arrow set as he gets closer, then

Toffs in the Tenement

I look to my right and standing at the next close is the wee boy who tried to give the t-shirt of his back to the Ragman.

I beckon to the wee boy with my hand to come over, he gestures back with two fingers, I beckon again with more conviction, mouthing the words "Come Here", the wee boy slowly walks over with an apprehensive look on his face, and asks "Whit ur ye wanting?", "Here" I say, pushing the bow and arrow into his hands, while looking over his shoulder at Father getting ever closer, the wee boy's face lights up in disbelief as he says "Ta ", and runs off to show his pals his new bow and arrow set.

Just then father arrives at the close looking exasperated, "All the shops are closed",he tells me, as if it is something I should be concerned about "I'm going to have to go to the Barra's", he exclaims, "What for?", I find myself asking, "A mop", he answers, as if it was obvious, he then puts his hand on my shoulder and ushers me towards the stairs, as we head up the stairs, to my relief, I cant hear anyone on our landing, but as we pass the toilet Fathers face screws up, someone is really having a torrid time of it as the same grunts, groans and smells are escaping from under the toilet door just like they did earlier on, we both hold our noses with two fingers as we carry on up the stair and into our house.

As we enter the house Mother is messing about with the net curtain on the window, "I'm sorry Rupert I couldn't find any rags", she says, while continuing to fuss with the curtain "That's okay", I reply hiding my red face behind an old commando comic that was lying on the couch, "I think we need a new curtain", she continues, "Well", Father says "In that case I think we should all go to the Barra's".

Mother hates the Barra's, over the last two years we must have been about twenty times, and each and every time we go through the same rigmarole, it starts with her saying "What if I meet somebody I know?" then Father has to respond with "If you did meet someone you know, they would be thinking the exact same thing about you", to which she will reply "I better put on my good clothes just in case".

Mother always goes to the Barra's looking very posh, hat, jewellery the lot. She likes the fact that all the stallholders at the Barra's fawn over her because they think she has money, if possible, she also takes a five pound note, if she has five single pound notes, poor father has to go to a shop and get them changed into a five pound note so that she can bring it out of her purse and announce, in her poshest voice, to the poor stallholder "This is the smallest note I have, do you have enough change?", even if the item she is buying only costs 3d.

Toffs in the Tenement

After we have gone through all the usual procedures, Mother is fully dressed, she has her five pound note in her purse, and we are just about ready to go when the front door swings open and in storms Wilhelmina," What is that smell on the landing" she proclaims, "And those noises" she continues before noticing mother is dressed in her Sunday clothes putting the finishes touches to her lipstick at the mirror on the wall. "Where are you all going?" she asks, "We are going to the Barrows" Mother replies, drawing a smirk from Father and me "What about me?", Wilhelmina queries, "You're very welcome to come with us to the Barra's", Father offers, quite chuffed that he said Barra's, but still draws a stern glance from Mother for inadvertently correcting her pronunciation.

Just then there is a knock at the front door, "I'll get it" I shout, making my way to the door, as I open the door Sammy is standing there with his gun in one hand and two fingers of the other hand over his nose, "Ur ye comin'oot tae play?" he asks in a high pitched squeaky voice due to the fact he is pinching his nose, "Whit izat smell?" he adds ,still sounding like Pinky and Perky, "I can't , I'm going to the Barra's" I answer, " Kin ah cum ?" asks Sammy, I turn around and shout to father " Can Sammy come with us to the Barra's?", "Of course", Father replies, "Just quickly check with Sammy's parents" he adds.

As we start to head down the stairs en route to Sammy's we can hear the toilet flushing, we pause for a moment as the toilet door opens, in anticipation of finding out who the smelly person is, a big hand appears holding a Daily record, then a big belly, finally we see Mr Campbell, he stands on the landing after closing the toilet door and proclaims "Ahhh, that's better", while pulling the back of his trousers from his bottom. He spots Sammy and me and announces proudly "Ah must be aboot a stone lighter eh lads?" as he walks past us on the stairs and into his house.

We run to Sammy's house and get permission from his parents for him to join us on our trip to the Barra's, and as we are walking back to my close we can hear shouting coming from Mr and Mrs Campbell's house through their open window, "Whit dae ye bloody mean sumdys knocked ma' claes?" Mr Campbell screeches, I can only presume that Mrs Campbell has just informed him of the events of earlier on , "Ah need tae change ma troosers" he yells, At this point I explain the situation to Sammy regarding the earlier mix up with the rags, who rather than sympathise with my plight proceeds to burst out laughing.

We enter my close and climb the stairs , Sammy is still laughing at my misfortune when we reach the landing , we can now clearly hear the furore coming from next door, "If ah catch ra bastard rat stole ma claes ah'll pit ma toe up his erse" rants Mr Campbell, " aye if ye kin stay oot ra shitehoose long enough " taunts Mrs Campbell ,this statement just sends Sammy over the edge and he is now doubled up with laughter sitting on the top stair of our landing, with tears running down his face, although I am trying my best not to laugh, I find myself slowly joining in with Sammy, and start to snigger, before long I cant hold back anymore and I start to laugh out loud.

We are still laughing when Mother, Father and Wilhelmina come out the house, Wilhelmina has changed her clothes and now looks like a miniature version of Mother, Father is in the process of locking our door, when Mr Campbell races out of his house and down the stair to the toilet, we quickly make our way down the stair so that we are not subjected to the smell and noises about to emanate from the toilet.

At the bottom of the stairs we bump into Old Mrs Mc Lean she is tottering up and down the close bending over every now and again looking at the ground, "Have you lost something Mrs Mc Lean?"

Father asks, "Aye ah huv " snaps Mrs Mc Lean, thinking it must be a ring or a necklace father then says "Would you like us to give you a hand to look " "Aye " Mrs Mc Lean answers, so we all bend over looking at the ground when mother asks "What did you drop Mrs Mc Lean?", "A STITCH " Mrs Mc Lean cackles as she heads into her house laughing at our naivety, Mother straightens up and glares in Mrs Mc Lean's direction not appreciating the humour, " Witch " Wilhelmina mumbles under her breath.

Sammy and I are a few steps ahead of the rest of the family as we near the last close in Heron st, we look over at Mrs Mc Kay's house expecting her to be at her window as usual, but to our surprise there is no-one there, we edge closer to the window to investigate this phenomenon, when up she pops, frightening the living daylights out of me and Sammy, who jump back and nearly fall off the pavement, "Ah drapped ma biscuit", she proclaims, showing us a custard cream.

As she assumes her usual position at the window, the rest of the family have caught up with us, "Whaur ur yeez awe gon ra day then?" enquires Mrs Mc Kay, "We are heading for the Ba..." Father is interrupted by a dig in the ribs from Mother, "We are heading into town to do a bit of shopping", Mother replies, as we continue on our journey, "Enjoy the Barra's then", Mrs Mc Kay shouts behind us, "We will", Mother replies, before stopping as she realises what she has just said, Mrs McKay has a good chuckle at our expense, Mother on the other hand lifts her nose in the air before declaring "Stupid woman", and leading us on our way towards Bridgeton cross.

Bridgeton cross (Toll)was a totally different place on a Sunday, it was like a ghost town, all the shops are closed , as are all the pubs, the traffic is non existent except for the odd bus now and again. We cross over the Toll and make our way down London Rd, where we join the small, but constant, procession of people heading towards the Barra's, five minutes later, after crossing Abercrombie St, the entrance to the Barra's is only fifty yards in front of us, the first thing I notice is the crowds all slowly walking through the bottleneck entrance, the noise of people shouting trying to sell their goods can be heard from all over the area surrounding the Barra's, the smell of tobacco, fish and doughnuts fills the air, as we all hold on to each other and join the throng of people slowly moving through the entrance.

If you have never visited the Barra's before, the first time can be quite daunting; I can clearly remember my first visit. The Barra's is made up of indoor and outdoor markets with what seems like hundreds of stalls, they sell anything and everything at the Barra's, but there was this one stall I particularly remember, it was run by this old hag of a woman, she must have been about eight-five years old, stick thin with no teeth, except two at the front. She wore this sort of money belt/ apron type thing, were she would stand with her hands inside the pocket of her apron jingling all the change. Her hands were very thin and bony, partly covered with black fingerless woolly gloves.

But it was her stall that fascinated me, it contained items advertised, on a hand written piece of card cut from a cornflakes box, as antiques. Things like brass jugs with dents in them, necklaces with enormous different coloured pearls, old musty books with the covers hanging off with titles like "Surgery for beginners" in gold leaf writing, and "I built the Drummochter pass" by Professor Cecil Bartholomew Hume , I wondered to myself "who would buy this stuff", but what makes this stall stick in my mind to this day, was in amongst all these so called antiques, there was always a pile of LPs, and the LP at the top of the pile was always a "Top of the pops" LP.

I remember I picked up an old pen from her stall as Father looked at one of her books, "How much is this",I asked, holding up the pen, " 'Ats an antique pen" she cackled, sounding like a pantomime witch, "That belanged tae Archduke thingy ma bobby, when he wiz shot in Sara whitsitsname",she continued "So how much is it", I asked again, "A tanner", she replied, her eyesight must have been extremely bad as well, because down the side of the pen it read "City cash tailors" I chuckled to myself at the thought of Archduke Ferdinand coming to Glasgow with a Provvie cheque to buy a suit, and swiftly returned the pen to the stall.

Anyway, once we are through the entrance the crowd disperses in all directions looking for bargains, Mother and Wilhelmina spot the stall with the net curtains, while father, Sammy and me all head to the stalls indoors, we agree to meet up again outside the whelk shop on London rd in an hour.

Once inside the smell hits you straight away, it's a mixture of fried food and stale tobacco there is a cloud of tobacco smoke hovering over our heads, which is being added to all the time by the stallholder's cigarettes, pipes and cigars. The stalls inside are joined together in straight lines the full width of the building with an aisle between them, allowing people to walk up and down between the stalls. There is everything you could imagine on sale from stags heads to paper clips.

Father drags us over to this stall that sells hats, "Ur ye looking furra a nice bunnet sir?", asks the fat man working behind the stall, as Sammy and I look on, Father picks up a flat cap and tries it on "I could be doing with a new hat", Father informs Billy Bunter behind the stall, Now father has never worn any type of hat in his life, this is his attempt to look like all the other working class men in Bridgeton who all seem to own a bunnet, the cap he tries on is sitting on top of his head and is blatantly far too small, "Fits ye like a glove sir", says the fat man unconvincingly, Father turns round to face Sammy and me while still trying to pull down this cap, "what do you think lads ?" he asks "Aye" is Sammy's short response as he fidgets uncomfortably, I feel on the other hand that I cant let this potential sale go through as he looks stupid, "It looks a bit small", is my reply, Fatty behind the stall glares right at me, as if he wants to kill me, "We dae huv 'ris ither larger cap sir", says fatty, emphasising the word larger for my behalf, Father tries this one on and it falls over his ears and eyes and sits on his nose, "Rat's much better sir, as if it wiz made fur ye I'd say", observes fatty, Father turns once again to me and Sammy, "well what do you think of this one lads?" He gets the usual "Aye" from Sammy, "It's far too big for you", I suggest immediately, looking at fatty as I speak, well, after hearing this fatty is about to blow a gasket, "Ye dae need plinty o' room coz yer heed kin swell in the heat", was fatty's final desperate attempt to land this sale, "I'll just leave it thank you", Father decides, as he puts the cap back on the fat mans stall. "Nae problem sir", fatty replies through gritted teeth, while glaring at me, as we walk away both Sammy and me stick our tongues out at fat man, who to our complete surprise, sticks his tongue out back at us, as this was totally unexpected, we are taken aback, until Sammy says "Ignore him, he's jist a big wean", and we march away following Father through the crowds.

Father stops at a stall that is selling household goods, mops, brushes, dusters etc, he starts to rummage through all the goods on display, when I notice the stall next to it sells toys, I point this out to Sammy who's eyes light up as we attack the bundles of cheap plastic toys on display, there are rubber snakes , a multitude of plastic guns, super balls, plasticine and loads of other great stuff.

I lift up a plastic face mask of a werewolf and try it on, through the eye holes I notice the stall opposite which sells second hand clothes, and there searching through the jumble of clothes is Mrs Campbell, she lifts up a pair of trousers and asks "Much dae ye want fur these?" still looking through the mask I lower my eyes to the owner of the stall , who is sitting down drinking a cup of tea, I gulp deeply as I recognise him , it's the Ragman from earlier on today, "Ten bob", he replies to Mrs Campbell, I move the mask back up towards Mrs Campbell and notice the trousers she is holding have a snake belt in the waistband, I gulp even deeper, and the blood drains from my face, when after thinking for a couple of seconds she announces "Ah'll take thum, but at ten bob ye should be wearin' a mask ya money grabbing bastard", she throws a ten bob note grudgingly on the stall and rolls the trousers up and puts them in her string bag, as she walks away from the stall.

I slowly lower the mask from my face, "You look as if yiv seen a ghost", Sammy observes as he sees my chalk white face, "Mrs Campbell has just bought her own trousers", I mutter, "Whit dae ye mean?", asks Sammy, "Eh! Never mind", I say, as I decide to forget all about Mrs Campbell's trousers, "What's that you've got there", I ask Sammy, "Stink bombs", Sammy replies with a wicked glint in his eye.

We both empty our pockets as we intend to pool our resources to make this purchase, and after close inspection of the contents we have a sum total of two elastic bands, five jorries, a set of five stones, a whistle, two pieces of half eaten chewing gum and thruppence ha'penny cash, "We're tuppence ha'penny short",Sammy concludes, "leave it to me",I announce confidently.

I squeeze in beside father through a crowd of people at the household goods stall, where he is holding a mop head in one hand, and a long wooden pole in the other, the confused expression on his face suggests that joining the two items together isn't going to come easy for him, I tug on his jacket to get his attention, and when he turns round the pole he is holding whizzes over my head missing me by about half an inch, "Ah Rupert ,I have bought the mop for mother", he says, proud of his achievement, I put on my best begging voice and ask "Can I have tuppence ha'penny please father?" , "It's for a science experiment at school",I add quickly, to lend weight to my request. "I was never any good at science", he replies, stating what I already knew, before adding "What do you want to buy?", after thinking for a minute I proclaim in a knowledgeable manner, "It's for a small box of pellets, that once broken, create a chemical reaction with the air, then we have to write a detailed report on that reaction", Father now has an even more confused look on his face, "I see", he says, trying to give the impression he knows what I'm talking about, he puts his hand in his pocket ,while I hold the mop head, he then hands me tuppence ha'penny and I hand him back the mop head. "What are these pellets called?" he asks, as I turn to make my way back to Sammy, "eh! Repugnant aroma capsules", I answer quickly, "Oh! Stink bombs", Father says, as I stop in my tracks and turn to face him, he just winks at me and says "Don't let your Mother see them".

After purchasing the stink bombs with Sammy, we join Father, and head off to meet Mother and Wilhelmina at the whelk shop. The Barra's is absolutely packed with people when we get outside, there are stallholders shouting, people talking, children screaming, music blaring, and the smell of food is everywhere, the stall holders near the entrance of the Barra's have attracted large crowds with their sales patter, there are cries of "Two furra pound, two furra pound", and "Not five pounds, not even four pounds, my wife will kill me for giving them away, but three pounds for this lovely set of towels".

There is a one man band busking in the middle of the road banging his drums and blowing his kazoo, a drunk man has decided to start dancing to his jaunty tunes, holding a quarter bottle of whisky in the air, entertaining an appreciative audience with his antics, the ground is covered with litter, there is discarded paper left by people eating chips, doughnuts and whelks, and plastic cups of various sizes which are being blown about by the wind down these narrow streets.

We squeeze our way through the throngs of people and I notice Father is the only one with manners saying "Excuse me", as he slides between the mass of bodies, everyone else is just pushing their way through, eventually we reach a small pocket of space, after looking around like a periscope, Father announces "There's your Mother and Wilhelmina at the curtain stall up ahead", he then grabs my hand and drags me in the direction of the curtain stall, poor Sammy is trying to keep up ,and all I can hear behind me is him squealing "Ouch", as people stand on his feet, while we are squeezing through the crowd.

We arrive at the curtain stall just in time to hear mother saying "I believe we will need between fifteen and twenty yards of material young man" the lad behind the stall starts feverishly measuring out fifteen yards of material using a yardstick, he has a big smile on his face at the prospect of such a large sale, this is when Wilhelmina plays her part in this subterfuge to perfection, "I think we better make sure it matches first Mother", Wilhelmina suggests right on cue, "Your quite right dear", says Mother "How much do you think we will need to check if it matches?" she asks Wilhelmina, "I think one yard should do it Mother" says Wilhelmina "And we can check it matches all the rooms in the house", she adds, at this point the lad behind the stall is devastated and glares at Wilhelmina , he stretches one length of material against the yard stick, marks and cuts it , he then places it in a brown bag and hands it to Mother, "Two bob" he says with a fake smile on his face, Father and me know what is about to happen, Mother opens her purse and hands the lad a five pound note saying "This is the smallest note I have do you have enough change", at this point Sammy is extremely impressed, "Wow" he gushes "Ur yoos rich?", he adds, the curtain stall lad hands over nearly all his loose change to her, with a look of exasperation on his face, she carries on the charade by saying "If this matches all the rooms in the house we will come back for the rest", I had to laugh at the "all the rooms in the house statement" one window in a single end.

As we all stand in a group deciding what to do next, a tramp approaches Mother and asks "kin ye spare a penny furra cup o' tea?" She looks at the tramp lifts her nose in the air and says "Go away", the tramp is persistent and asks again "C'mon ye must huv a penny tae spare?" Mother then turns her back on us , so we can't hear her , leans over to the tramp and through gritted teeth warns "If ye don't bugger off ah'll get ye lifted by the polis?" the poor tramp just didn't expect that response from such a well dressed woman "Ah liked ye better wi the brush up yer arse" he retorts before slinking away to annoy someone else, Mother turns back to us "Right who would like some whelks?" she asks, back to her posh best, "Ah don't like wulks, they look like snotters" Sammy says, bringing a smile to father and me's face,"I don't like them either", Wilhelmina announces while doing a fake shiver at the thought, "How about chips?" Father asks "yeah" we all say at the same time, "Chips it is then" Father concludes, as we head to the chip shop on the Gallowgate.

Toffs in the Tenement

When we arrive at the chip shop there is a small queue in front of us and I notice there is a small lady working behind the counter, you can hardly see her for the glass covered area where the cooked food is kept warm, she seems to be under a bit of pressure, as we join the end of the queue, she stands on her tip toes and shouts to Mother "Am sorry hen we're waiting oan chips", there is steam rising from the deep fat fryers as a large basket full of uncooked chips is poured into the boiling fat, this is followed by the loud sound of sizzling and crackling coming from the now cooking chips ,the smell of stale fat fills the air, and the tobacco stained yellow walls could do with a lick of paint.

The shop itself is quite long with the serving counter at the far end, on the right hand side is a seating area with six Formica topped tables with bench style seating running along the right hand wall, of which two of them are empty, mother spots the empty tables and after getting over being called "Hen" by the small lady behind the counter, suggests we sit in for our chips.

Mother, Father and Wilhelmina slide into one table as me and Sammy slide in to the one behind them, Sammy and I immediately grab a menu each and discuss what we are going to have, meanwhile at Mothers table a young waitress has approached and asks "Whit ye wanting" she must have been about the same age as Wilhelmina, but that is where any comparison ends, she was chewing gum while scratching her head with her pencil, her uniform consisted of black everything, with a dirty white apron, she also gave the impression that she would rather be somewhere else. Mother looks at the menu, as our waitress stands beside her tapping her pencil on her pad, "Is it haddock or cod you serve here?" she asks, "Uh" the waitress replies, obviously never having been asked that question before "What type of fish do you serve here?" Mother asks again, the waitress thinks for a moment then answers "Ordinary and special", Mother gives up, shaking her head she resigns herself to the fact that she is fighting a lost cause "Three fish teas and two plates of chips" she says as she puts the menu back in the holder, "Dae ye want anyfing tae drink?", our waitress asks, "Irn-bru", me and Sammy shout in unison. Mother acknowledges to the waitress that the irn bru can be added; she scribbles on her pad and slopes off.

As we are waiting on our chips, Sammy and me are listening to the of the old couple sitting at the table in front of us, they are slurping their tea out of a saucer, and trying to eat their food with no teeth, " Kin a' dip ma chip in yer egg?" the old man asks, "bugger off" replies the old woman, moving her plate closer to her, "Is that a spider oan rat wa'behind ye?"

asks the old man, "where", the old woman replies turning round quickly, and as she does, the old man makes his move and dips his chip in the woman's fried egg, as she turns back round she notices the egg has been breached, and looking at the old man she moans "Ya durty bastard, ye dipped it didn't ye?" "Naw a never", he replies, with egg yoke running down his chin, "Aye ye did ya bugger" she insists, "If that's ra way ye want tae play it" she adds, she then dips two chips in his tea and then eats them, the old man looks at his tea which now has a layer of grease floating on it, "Right narket noo", the old man pleads, "That's enough, ah take ye oot furra nice meal and rat's whit ye dae tae me", he adds, "Ach, slurp yer tea and sook yer chips," the old woman replies. Sammy and I are giggling at their antics, when our waitress arrives with five plates balanced on her two arms, she is followed by a clone carrying the tea, as the waitress sets the plates down, her clone asks "who's ra' irn bru fur?", Sammy and me put our hands up just like we do in school when the teacher asks a question, "Do you have any napkins?" Mother asks, the waitress and her clone look at each other, before Mother says "Never mind", and pulls a small pack of handkerchiefs out of her bag and distributes them to everybody.

After we have finished, Father pays the bill, and the rest of us get ready to leave, as we head for the door our waitress announces in a mock posh voice "I do hope you enjoyed your meal",Mother turns round and glares at the waitress, who pretends to be busy "bitch" Wilhelmina mutters as we leavethe chip shop.

As we stand outside the chip shop on the Gallowgate Father is struggling to carry the pole and mop he bought, when a man shouts "Alright Bert?", from across the road, Mother looks at Father and repeats "Bert", he smiles bashfully and says "I'll explain later", as he crosses the road to speak to the man.

The rest of us decide its time to head home, but not before Mother and Wilhelmina have a look inside a shop called Reeta's, this is a woman's clothes shop, so me and Sammy are ordered to wait outside as they enter the shop, while we are standing outside the shop we can see Father and the other guy in deep conversation across the road, then Sammy says to me "Ah'll be back in a minute, am gon tae use ra' toilet in the chip shop" he walks the ten yards to the chip shop and disappears inside, and I am left standing alone outside Reeta's, I'm considering moving along to the tool shop a couple of doors down, when Sammy returns with a big smile on his face, before I can ask him what he is smiling about, Mother and Wilhelmina come out of Reeta's declaring they will return next week when they can take their time and have a good look without us guys holding them back.

All of a sudden we can hear a commotion coming from the chip shop "Fur Christ's sake rat's honking" shouts one man as he exits the chip shop, "that's disgusting" moans the old woman as she leaves, followed by the old man groaning "Jeezo that's boufing",before long the chip shop is emptied including the staff, as they all stand in the street coughing and spluttering, I look at Sammy, who's grin is even wider than before, "Serves thum right fur rur cheek", he declares, while trying to stuff the remaining stink bombs in his pocket. After five minutes the people start to go back in the chip shop, Sammy and I are still laughing at their misfortune, when Father arrives back from his conversation with the mystery man, "Great news everybody" he declares "What", we all say at the same time, he looks at everyone for what seams like ages , then announces "WE'RE FLITTING".

Toffs in the Tenement

Ra' Nairn's ur flittin'

When Father told us a couple of days ago at the Barra's, in his best Bridgeton brogue, that we were flitting, my sister Wilhelmina's face lit up, I hadn't seen her smile like that since I fell four feet head first out of our recess bed ,when she let go the duffle coat we were fighting over ,she immediately thought about having her own room again, a large bathroom, back and front garden, shopping in Byres Rd, but her smile soon changed to a pained expression when she heard we were only moving to a room and kitchen, right next door to our single end.

It was if someone had took a hundred yard run up and booted her right in the stomach, "Noooo" she whined, as she stared into space, "Noooo" she continued whining, as she walked zombie like in no particular direction. When I look at Wilhelmina now, she has calmed down, and, as we help Mother pack our things for the big move, to my dismay, she has started to speak coherently again and has stopped slabbering and whining. Mother's attitude to the move was one of optimism and pessimism, she sees it as a step in the right direction, as two rooms are an improvement on one, but as we haven't yet been inside the room and kitchen we are moving into in only two days, she is dreading the work involved, painting, decorating, cleaning etc, so she has enlisted the help of our next door neighbour Mrs Campbell at a negotiated rate of five shillings, with the payment upfront of course.

As we all wait on Father returning with the keys to our new flat, I am busy fishing out my stuff from under the recess bed, Wilhelmina is sitting on the couch looking at an old Bunty annual filled with scraps, scraps are little paper cut outs of angels ,brides , grooms etc, which are kept flat between the pages of a book, girls then swap them with their friends, it doesn't take

Toffs in the Tenement

Wilhelmina long to browse through her collection though, as her so called friends have swapped all her good scraps for chubby angels on blue and pink clouds, she slams the book closed and tosses it in a box. Mother and Mrs Campbell are preparing all the cleaning materials that are going to be needed to make our new flat habitable, and as I look at poor Mrs Campbell she resembles a pack mule in a cowboy film, she has dusters over her shoulders, a basin and chamois in one hand, and a mop and bucket in the other, she also has a variety of cloths under her arm, Mother on the other hand only has a pair of rubber gloves in her hand, "If ye stick a brush up ma' arse I'll sweep the close as well" Mrs Campbell moans, Mother takes the hint and removes the cloths from Mrs Campbell's arms and shoulder, "Aye, rat's much better", says Mrs Campbell sarcastically, while raising her eyes to the heavens and making a huffing noise.

At this point I am packing my Johnny Seven rifle in a box, when my mind drifts towards Mr and Mrs Cowan the young couple who ,up until two weeks ago, stayed in the flat we were moving into, they were a very mysterious couple, but very nice, Mrs Cowan was a very pretty lady with blonde hair, blue eyes and a cheery smile, she was always very well dressed, but you never saw her hanging out a washing, or speaking to the other neighbours ,in fact, she very rarely left her flat, Mother and Mrs Campbell were always talking about her, but for different reasons, Mother was quite jealous of Mrs Cowan's clothes and recognised that they were from expensive shops, she also didn't like the fact that Mrs Cowan spoke properly, as she liked being the only 'snob' in this street.

Mrs Campbell on the other hand had a very different reason for not liking Mrs Cowan, I heard her talking to Mr Campbell in the back court on the day the Cowan's moved in "Rat's awe ah need, two snobby bastards oan ma' landing", she moans. I personally, really liked Mrs Cowan, she used to ask me and my pal Sammy to go to the shops for her, which we always loved to do as she would give us a shilling each, it used to drive mother crazy trying to figure out where they got their money from because no-one knew what Mr Cowan did for a living.

You only ever saw the enigmatic Mr Cowan at night when he left his house, if I was playing in the close, he would always stop and ask how I was getting on at school, or did I have a girlfriend yet, before jumping in a fancy waiting car and speeding off, he wouldn't return home until the early hours of the morning, and the reason I know this is ,I sometimes wake up in the early hours of the morning absolutely freezing because Wilhelmina has pulled all the bedclothes and coats over to her side of the bed, and at that time in the morning it is very quiet, so while I'm in the process of reclaiming my share of the bedclothes, I would hear the sound of a car door slamming on the street below our window, and footsteps coming up the stair, I would then hear Mrs Cowan opening the door and welcoming Mr Cowan home ,they would then shut the door behind them, which was followed by the noise of a succession of locks being closed that would last for what seemed like five minutes. I imagined he was secret agent like James Bond and was returning from secret missions, but I would snigger to myself at the thought of a S.P.E.C.T.R.E. agent from the Calton, trying to take over the world.

Mr Cowan was also a lot younger than Father, and like Mrs Cowan, always had the latest fashionable clothes, he looked like the actor Tony Curtis, and Mother would tease Father by commenting on how good looking Mr Cowan was, "If I was ten years younger",she would say, but for some reason she never elaborated on that statement, so I never found out what would happen if she was ten years younger.

Father would always retort in a snobbish manner "The wine tastes better from older casks", before lifting his opened newspaper up in front of his face forming a barrier between Mother and him.

Mr and Mrs Cowan had only stayed in the flat for about three months, and no-one saw or heard them move out, Mrs Campbell made sure we all knew her theory at the time, when she declared "The bastards musta' dun a moonie", I later found out a moonie meant a moonlight flit, this involves moving out of your house in the middle of the night without telling anyone, it is usually done if you owed rent money, Father has since informed us, that his friend at the rent office told him that Mrs Cowan had paid their rent up until the end of the month, and had left a letter for the landlord, who was on holiday at the moment, which only added to the mystery.

Another reason Mrs Campbell took an instant dislike to the Cowan's right away, was because Mr Campbell was always offering to help Mrs Cowan with any odd jobs she needed done, but she never took him up on his kind offers, and in Mrs Campbell's own words "He wiz following hur aboot like a wahlly dug ", I wish I knew what a wahlly dug was, but I am sure it is a derogatory term.

When the Cowan's first moved in there was a flurry of activity for a while with a lot of people coming and going, men arrived with big boxes, other men would arrive with tool bags and the sound of hammering and banging reverberated throughout the close, this drove Mrs Campbell mad ,she would often be heard shouting at the workmen "Fur Christ's sake geezabrek wi' rat racket, ma man's oan ra nightshift",this would be followed by Mr Campbell shouting back from the outside toilet "Am ur not oan ra nightshift ya lying old witch", just in case Mrs Cowan was listening and needed his services in the future.

To everyone's relief, after a couple of days the banging stopped, but no-one from up the close has ever been inside the Cowan's flat to see what the banging was all about or what was in those boxes, which again added to the anticipation of Father returning with the keys.

"Hello everyone", Father announces cheerily as he enters the flat, "Hello", we shout back, even more cheerily, in unison, except Mrs Campbell who mutters under her breath "Christ's sake, am gonny be sick", "Pardon?", Mother asks, looking daggers at Mrs Campbell ,"Nuhin'", Mrs Campbell replies nervously while lowering her head and trying to look busy fiddling with her mop and bucket, Mother glares at her for a couple of seconds then turns her attention to Father. "Well, did you get them?" she asks Father abruptly, when he is finished hanging up his coat up on the hooks in our small hall, he starts to fiddle about in the pockets of his coat, he then spins round and shouts "Tarrah", as he jingles a set of keys in his hand,"yeah" we all shout, and for some obscure reason we also break into applause, as I stare at the keys I can see that there are seven keys in the set, and think to myself "That is a lot of locks for one door", we only had one key for our door, "Right, who's ready to go and see our new flat?"Father asks excitedly, as he pretends to run towards our front door, we all rush to the front door as well, and in the stampede poor Mrs Campbell stands on her mop bucket and falls backwards onto the couch where she lands on a pile of Fathers Frank Sinatra L.P.s she then continues to slide off the couch and lands on the floor with a thud, "Ah ma' arse", she screams, as she sits on the floor propped up against the couch like a puppet who's strings have been cut.

Mother and Father rush over to help her back to her feet, and as they gingerly lift her up by the arms, Wilhelmina and me are trying to stifle our giggles, Mrs Campbell notices our poor attempt to hide our laughter and looks directly at us and states "Je hink rats funny?" the obvious answer would have been Yes, but we manage to shake our heads to indicate No," Aye, bloody right its no funny" she retorts, "If it wisnae fur ma' fat arse rat wid huv been a right sore yin", she concludes , on hearing this statement Wilhelmina and I both turn round and bite the recess curtains to control our laughter, Mrs Campbell regains her composure and gathers up her cleaning equipment then hobbles towards the front door.

As we stand there in a line outside our new flat, Sammy appears at the top of the stairs "Hi Rupert "he says "Whit's gon oan?" he asks, I explain the situation to him as he joins me in the queue for our new flat and we watch Father struggling to work out what key fits what lock, "Yer da's goat mer keys rin the janny at ma'school", Sammy comments with a smile, Father eventually unlocks one, then two, by now we are all standing as if we need the toilet, in anticipation, "Hurry up Father", Wilhelmina begs, jumping up and down on the spot, locks three four and five follow in quick succession, "Come on Hubert" Mother says quickly, trying to appear calm, lock six opens , and as Father inserts the key in the last lock, Mr Campbell appears from his flat with a newspaper under his arm, "Je get yer keys then?" he enquires as he makes his way down the stairs to the toilet, "Naw,thur brekkin' in ya bammy bastard" answers his wife sarcastically, he shakes his head in despair, as he disappears into the sanctuary of the toilet, Mrs Campbell then advises everyone "Ah'd get in rer quick afore he starts shiting",Mother looks at her in disbelief, and is in the process of shaking her head at Mrs Campbell's antics when there is a clicking noise and lock seven opens.

Father hesitantly pushes the door and it slowly swings open, "Wow", Father exclaims, "Wow", Mother concurs, at this point the rest of us still can't see past them "What, what", we shout together, as Father and Mother slowly enter the hall of the flat we quickly move forward and stand at the door "Jeezo", Mrs Campbell comments, as she looks over the heads of Wilhelmina, me and Sammy, the small hall was absolutely stunning, it had a brass coat stand and empty mahogany bookcase, it looks as if it has just been decorated, with plain wallpaper above a wooden rail that runs the length of the hall about four feet above the skirting, it has candy striped wallpaper below the rail, and a lovely red carpet, "Rat's ra best loaby av ever seen", says Sammy obviously very impressed, Father has now entered through the door to the front room, and the 'wow' factor continues, the wooden rail, the carpet, and full length curtains, there is a stunning black leather three piece suite and mahogany coffee table, there is also a beautiful long mirror on the wall, by this time Mrs Campbell has left the cleaning equipment at the front door, as it wont be needed ,and as she looks around the front room, she mutters "Ya jammy bastards", The window is absolutely spotless as we open the curtains, the light floods in illuminating the whole room and dazzles our eyes when it reflects off the glass front of a small bar sitting in the corner, the fireplace has been replaced with a gas fire, and there is an empty TV cabinet in the corner next to the window, sitting next to the TV cabinet is a radiogram, a combined radio and record player in a lovely mahogany cabinet, "Ya durty jammy bastards" Mrs Campbell mumbles again.

Mother and Father make there way to the back room and open the door, it is just as impressive as the front room, there is even kitchen cabinets on the walls, as well as a new gas cooker, at the sink there is a geyser that dispenses hot water, and you have a cracking view from the back window right across the Booly to London Rd, this room also has a gas fire, and the bed recess has a full length red velvet curtain pulled right, across concealing whatever is behind it.

Mother walks over to the curtain and opens it fully, and all our jaws drop to the floor, Mrs Campbell mutters "Ya durty...." Mother interrupts with "I know, jammy bastards", without even realising what she is saying, as we all stare in amazement we are joined by Wilhelmina and Father, "Wow", Father exclaims again, Wilhelmina screeches, one word at a time, "Oh-My-God". As we all continue to gazin disbelief, an unfamiliar voice from behind us asks "Dae ye like oor bathroom then?",there is a moments silence before we all slowly turn round to find Mr Cowan standing there smiling, he is then joined by a group of men, "Ah bult rat", one of the men announces proudly, he is referring to the lovely bathroom behind the recess curtain, there isn't anything plumbed in, but there is a sort of mahogany wooden cabinet that houses a shelf with a toilet seat on it, there is a large bucket with a lid below the toilet seat, next to the toilet is a cabinet with a porcelain jug and basin sitting on top of it, and finally, on the opposite wall is a solid, thick wooden frame about four feet tall ,which has three stairs leading to the top, where a full size bath with four cast iron legs is attached, there is a rolled up length of thin hose attached to the bottom of the bath where the plug hole is, which could be rolled out and put in the sink to drain the water from the bath ,it is also fully carpeted and has two wall lights with pull cords, one above the bath and one above the toilet."Ah put ra lights in", another man declares, obviously not wishing to be outdone.

We all listen intently as Mr Cowan explains that he has now moved to London after being promoted in his job as a croupier in a large casino in Glasgow city centre, he should have arrived yesterday to pick up the rest of his things, but his truck broke down at Carlisle, he also goes on to say that the bathroom was his wife's idea, and his four brothers, who are helping him today, are all tradesman in different trades so they built the bathroom for their sister in law, so she didn't have to go out at night to the outside toilet, while he was working at the casino, they also fitted extra locks on the door as Mrs Cowan was scared on her own.

As we return to our flat, leaving Mr Cowan and his brothers to get on with their removal, we all enter except Mrs Campbell, "Ah'm away hame ren, see yeez awe later", she says as she crosses the landing to her flat, "Ahem", Mother coughs, as she stands there with her hand out, rubbing her thumb against her index and middle finger, "Oh!, ra money rat's right, ah furgoat awe aboot rat there", Mrs Campbell pleads innocently, she places the five shillings into Mothers hand and storms off grumbling "Awe rat time n effort ,an awe ah end up wey izza sore erse".

Mother closes the front door behind her, still thinking about her lovely new flat, and with a spring in her step, heads over to the sink, grabbing the kettle en route, and starts to fill it with water, as she happily hums a song I've never heard of, Father starts to gather up his Frank Sinatra L.P.s, checking every one of them for any damage caused by the Mrs Campbell incident, and Wilhelmina slumps down on the couch and starts to read an old edition of the Mandy, everyone is very quiet when I break the silence and ask" can me and Sammy go out and watch the removal men?" Mother looks at Father and gives a barely noticeable shake of the head, then Father turns to me and says "You better not Rupert, you will just get in the way", on hearing Father's reply, Sammy looks at me and shrugs his shoulders, then asks me "dae ye want tae play boy, girl, fruit,?", I nod my head in agreement and make my way to the tallboy to get pencils and paper out of the top drawer.

Sammy taught me how to play boy girl fruit about a year ago, it involves drawing six columns on a piece of paper, each column has a different heading, boy, girl, fruit, animal, country and car, then you choose a letter of the alphabet, this is done by one person saying the alphabet to themselves, and the other person shouting STOP, whichever letter you stop at, you both have to come up with the name of a boy, girl fruit etc, starting with the chosen letter, after each round of letters you compare answers, if you both have the same answer you get five points, if you have different answers you get ten points, at the end of the game you add up the scores , the one with the highest score wins.

As we settle down to play on the floor at the front door, we can hear the shouts of "Left a bit, right a bit", coming from the landing, the youngest of the men seems to be slacking, and is getting a hard time, one of his brothers shouts "Pit yer back intae it ya lazy bastard", followed by another brother shouting, "I'll pit ma toe up yer arse if ye don't get ra finger oot", the poor lad resorts to his last line of defence when he shouts back" if any yoos touch me ah'll tell ma' maw", which seems to work as they back off saying " Well ,c'mon then jist hurry up".

Meanwhile back at our game Sammy has decided he will go first saying the alphabet, there is always an element of cheating when we play as Sammy only knows names for the letters A, B and C, and always starts at C,no matter when you say stop, as he shouts out "A", to let me know he has started saying the alphabet, I wait fully fifteen seconds before shouting "STOP", "C", he says unashamedly, and starts scribbling on his sheet of paper, now if he is only at C after fifteen seconds then at that rate it must take Sammy three quarters of an hour to say the whole alphabet. The reverse is true for me I have to say, as I know all the answers for the letters S,P, and W,so if its my go to say the alphabet and Sammy says" STOP" immediately after I shout "A" I always answer "W", which means I can say the full alphabet in about three eighths of a second.

After half an hour we are just about to add up the scores when there is a knock at the door, "I'll get it", I shout as I leap up and head for the door,, when I open the door Mr Cowan is standing there, "Hello Rupert, is yer da in?", he asks, Father has already heard him and comes to the door, "Here's yer keys back Mr Nairn, that's us off now "Mr Cowan says, as he hands Father back the keys, "cheerio then", Father replies, "Cheerio" Mother shouts from the background, Mr Cowan smiles at me as he ruffles my hair, turns and heads down the stairs to the waiting truck, what is it with adults and hair ruffling, they spend all day nagging you to comb your hair, then at the first available opportunity they ruffle it about with their hand, anyway, before Father can close the door, Mother runs over and says "Wait, lets go back in and have another look at the new flat", Father turns around and makes his way to the new flat next door, Sammy, Mother and me follow him, but Wilhelmina decides to stay and read her Mandy comic, Father makes short work of the locks this time and pushes open the door, "Oh" Father exclaims disappointedly, when he sees the coat stand and cabinet are gone,"Oh dear" Mother says, "the carpet's gone too ",she adds, they move towards the front room, and as they open the door they both stop dead in their tracks, the room has been gutted, no furniture or carpets, the gas fires are gone and so are the curtains, the room doesn't look anywhere near as appealing as it did earlier, Father then looks at Mother and they both proclaim at the same time " The back room".

They move as quick as they can through the hall and burst through the door of the back room, the room is totally bare, everything has been removed, the carpet, fire,geyser,cooker, even the kitchen cabinets, as they look behind them at the recess it is completely empty, the whole bathroom is gone even the thin hose and wall lights, the flat looks pretty grim now, and Mother is close to tears, "Ah well" says Father, as he puts his arm round Mother's shoulder, "At least it doesn't need decorated", he adds with a smile, Mother nods and we slowly all head back to our own flat.

The next day, Sammy and I are walking along Heron St heading towards the Dog Leg pub, on our way to Walters for sweets, when I hear a familiar voice shouting "Rupert", as I turn round I can see Mother hanging out of our window gesturing for me to return, I tell Sammy to wait, and run back towards the close, as I arrive beneath our first floor window, Mother asks me to get her a small bottle of disinfectant from Walters and throws a two shilling coin out of the window, as my eyes follow the coin in the air I am poised to catch it when I hear a woman's' voice saying "Hello Rupert", I automatically turn in the direction of the voice, and as I do, the coin bounces of the ground and stops at the feet of Mrs Cowan, as I stand there with a confused expression on my face, Mrs Cowan picks up the coin and hands it to me, she then looks up at Mother and waves, "Hello Mrs Nairn", she says, Mother partly waves back with a half smile on her face, she looks even more confused than me.

Just then a large truck turns into Heron St from Dalmarnock Rd and pulls up outside our close, by this time Sammy has joined me, Mrs Campbell has appeared at her window and Mrs Mc Kay at the bottom of the street has actually left her house and is standing on the pavement looking up at us desperately trying to see what is going on, two men get out of the truck and Mrs Cowan tells them to follow her as they enter the close and go up the stairs, Sammy and I follow them up to find out what is going on.

At the top of the stairs Mother has come out on the landing to meet Mrs Cowan, just as Mrs Campbell opens her door and stands there leaning against the opening, when Mrs Cowan reaches the landing with the two men Mother comments in a sarcastic tone "surely there cant be anything else left for you to take", Mrs Campbell adds "Mibee rer gonny strip the bloody paper aff ra woz", by this time Mrs Cowan looks utterly confused as she is about to put her key in the door, "What do you mean?" she asks, looking at Mother and continuing to open the door at the same time, before Mother can reply Mrs Campbell answers "yer man gutted ra place yisterday ya stupit bugger", "What" cries Mrs Cowan as she manages to open the door, she runs first into the front room ,then the back room, and as Mother and Mrs Campbell edge closer they can hear the sound of sobbing coming from the back room, they both quickly enter to find Mrs Cowan standing in the middle of the back room crying her eyes out with her hands covering her face, they both go over and each put an arm around Mrs Cowan, she stops crying long enough to tell Mother and Mrs Campbell that she left Mr Cowan two weeks ago after a big argument and moved back into her mothers house, they had been having some problems and she didn't want to move to London, so he went on his own, she left a letter at the rent office saying she would return before the end of the month to pick up her furniture, just as soon as she could find somewhere to store it , then the waterworks started again, "There, there" says Mother trying to console Mrs Cowan, "rer, rer", says Mrs Campbell , "he wiz an arsehole anyway ",she continues.

Toffs in the Tenement

Meanwhile the two removal men realise that they won't be removing anything and leave, Mother invites Mrs Cowan into our flat for a cup of tea, and Mrs Campbell returns to her flat, Sammy and me are left standing on the landing, and decide now would be a good time to try again and go to Walters for our sweets.

As we pass the Dog leg pub Mr Mc Kay staggers out on to the street, and nearly knocks us over, "Hullo rer Rueben "he slurs, as Sammy and me hold him up, "An wee Davis Jnr anaw ",he adds, looking at Sammy, "Our names are Rupert and Sammy Mr Mc Kay ", I say ,correcting his error "Whit ever", he slurs again, "Ah'm a wee bit taxi, kin ye get me a drunk?"He says while laughing to himself, he then straightens himself up using the wall for leverage and announces "Right, Ah'm now gone tae plant kisses oan ra wummin ah love" he says seriously, "Then Ah'm gon hame tae ra wife", he adds chuckling away merrily. We both watch as Mr Mc Kay staggers down Heron St, holding onto the wall to keep his balance, before bursting into song with a rousing rendition of High Noon.

We eventually reach Walter's, and as we enter Walter is in the middle of a one sided conversation with Mrs Cameron who lives up the next close to us at 45 Heron St, Mrs Cameron works in the Dog leg pub as a part time barmaid, she always wears a full length black cardigan that has seen better days, there are holes in the elbows and, it is that long she has to bend sideways to reach the pockets, it looks about ten sizes too big, as she tightly pulls one side over her chest from right to left, and the other side from left to right, until all you can see is a head and a two ankles with flat shoes attached, she now looks like a grub escaping from a black cocoon. She is telling Walter about one of the many incidents that take place during her shift, as Sammy and me wait patiently to be served, Mrs Cameron continues speaking at seventy miles an hour "An a said, whit ?" an she said " Ye did" an a said "Ah didnae" ren she says "did ye no'?"An a said "Naw" ren the cheeky cow says "Well a thought ye did "so ah jist said "Well, see whit thought done, peed ra bed an blamed it oan ra blanket" At this point Walter is losing the will to live, then Mrs Cameron finishes abruptly by saying "Christ Walter you kin talk fur Scotland, ah need tae get back tae ma work".

She then lifts the pint of milk she came in for off the counter and rushes out the shop, Walter is looking exasperated as he shakes his head from side to side and says "I huvnae goat a clue whit she wiz oan aboot" followed by "anyway whit kin a get fur yoos lads?" "Can I have a small bottle of disinfectant please" I say "An six penny dainties" Sammy adds, Walter hands over our purchases and we brace ourselves for the usual joke, and Walter didn't let us down, "By the way "he says "Did ye hear aboot the guy wi' nae ears that went blind?",he asks quizzically, "No" we reply, "His bunnet fell over his eyes" he answers, while laughing like a sea lion, Sammy and me pretend to laugh and leave the shop, safely outside Sammy moans " he's getting' wurse by the way" I nod in agreement as we make our way home, Twenty yards from the shop Mrs Cameron is standing talking to another woman, she has the bottle of milk she has just purchased cradled like baby in her arms, and as we get closer we can hear the familiar "Ren she said " "An ah jist said back" etc, the other woman was a lot more attentive than Walter was though, as she would know exactly when to butt in with a "Oh ah know" and "Rat's terrible".

We turn back into Heron St and head for my house, Mr Mc Kay is still trying to get home and is now using both hands against the wall to steady himself, as we pass him he is still singing at the top of his voice " Doooo not fur sake me oh ma' darlinnnnn'" he bellows, a wee boy shouts from his first floor window "yer singin's horrible mister", Mr Mc Kay answers quickly " no' as horrible as yer face'll be if a get ma hauns oan ye ya wee shite" while trying to locate the culprit by looking everywhere except up.

Sammy points to the bottom of the street and asks"izzat no' Mrs Cowan?", sure enough, I just catch sight of her before she disappears round the corner onto Dalmarnock Rd, "'Ats a shame, innit?" Sammy comments as we reach my close, as I know exactly what he is talking about I just nod, we deliver Mother's disinfectant and head back down the stairs, halfway down we can hear Mr Campbell in the toilet making noises as if he is trying to loosen a tight lid on a jar, we sit on the bottom stair and discuss what we are going to do next "whit aboot ra sonny pon?" Sammy suggests, the 'sonny pon' as Sammy calls it, are round shaped sand pits over in Glasgow Green, "I can't ", I reply, "my tea will be ready in an hour "I add to justify my decision, suddenly, there is an almighty crash coming from the toilet on the landing, this is followed by Mr Campbell shouting "Ah ya bastard", as we rush up the stair, water is gushing down the stairs from the toilet, Mother and Mrs Campbell have already come outside to investigate the noise, Mr Campbell appears from inside the toilet looking like a drowned rat, "Whit in gods name huv ye dun noo?" enquires Mrs Campbell from the landing, Mr Campbell looks up from the toilet landing, while standing there soaked from head to toe holding a piece of string " Ah only pullt the string tae flush ra bloody toilet "he replies "ra whole fing came aff ra wa' " he adds, , Sammy me and even Mother are trying our best not to laugh,"Ye'll need tae go roon tae ra factors and report it " Mrs Campbell moans, " get yer arse up here an get changed" she growls, as Mr Campbell slowly climbs the few stairs to his flat, his face is a deep red colour as every step is making a squidgy noise caused by the water seeping out of his wet slippers, it is only then that I realise the toilet probably won't be fixed tonight, and we will have to use the one upstairs which is even worse than ours.

Later that evening, as we are busy packing the remainder of our belongings for our move the next day, Father comes home and announces he has ordered linoleum for our new place, and bunk beds for Wilhelmina and me, which are all being delivered tomorrow, we both look at each other, but Wilhelmina beats me to the punch, "I want the top bunk", she shouts, as she sticks her tongue out me.

As I sit there resigned to the fact that I will be in the bottom bunk, but still pleased to be having my own bed, I look around our flat and the thought occurs to me that our single end doesn't look any bigger, even with all our belongings packed away in boxes and stored in the hall at the coal bunker, it is still a really tiny space for a family to live in, I wonder how the Mc Gowans who live above us cope in such a small space, as they have six children of various ages, I only have to put up with Wilhelmina, and it can be very difficult to find a private space in a single end if you don't want to speak to someone, I can only imagine that is why the streets are filled with children and adults from dusk till dawn , even if it's raining.

I am now feeling really excited about moving, but I am also a little bit sad, we have had a lot of good Halloweens here, and how much fun we had watching Mother trying to dook, and nearly impaling Fathers hand with a fork as he stirred the apples in the basin, as I look at Father sitting reading his newspaper, the slippers he is wearing remind me of Christmas, Mother bought the slippers for Father wrapped them up in lovely paper with a big bow and when he opened his beautifully wrapped gift on Christmas day he was delighted, until he tried them on, one slipper was a size nine and the other a size ten, he felt so sorry for Mother he never mentioned it and wears them to this day, I start to think off all the birthdays, Christmases and Halloweens and come to the conclusion that I have enjoyed living in this flat more than the big house in the west end, when I would hardly ever see Father because of his job, or Mother, who was always busy planning something.

As I get ready for bed for the last time in this single end, I suddenly remember that our toilet is broken and I will have to use the one upstairs, the toilet upstairs doesn't even have a lock on the door, there is no toilet seat, and there is a large hole in the corner where four bricks are missing and you can see right down to the back court, someone has stuffed newspapers in the hole but it is still absolutely freezing with the wind whistling through the makeshift repair, as I slowly climb the stairs trying to listen for evidence that the toilet is empty, I suddenly see Mr Campbell standing a couple of stairs from the toilet landing, he has a rolled up newspaper under his arm, but how on earth he was going to read it in the pitch dark I will never know, " Sumdys in" he says, nodding towards the toilet door, just then the toilet flushes, "izzit a pish or a shite?", he asks, looking at me right in the eye, " a pi.. A pee" I reply, embarrassingly correcting myself in the nick of time, "Aye, ye nearly said pish there dint ye?"He teases, while laughing at my expense, "On ye go "he adds, as one of the Mc Gowan clan rushes out of the toilet and up the stair carrying a now empty bucket, I successfully answer the call of nature and return to my flat and head straight to bed, all the memories have now been replaced with excitement and anticipation of our impending move.

In the morning I am awakened by a crashing noise followed by the sound of Father shouting "Ouch ", I open the bed recess curtain at the side and I can see Father jumping up and down in pain holding his foot, the big move has begun, I kick Wilhelmina in a crude attempt to wake her and shout excitedly " Time to get up, were flitting", as I pull open the curtains the light floods in and Wilhelmina moans "No, shout on me when its done", as she pulls the duffle coat back over her head, as I struggle to get dressed quickly, I notice that the bed settee is gone, and so have all the boxes, except the one Father has dropped on his foot, the front door is wide open and I can hear Mother in the new room and kitchen with Mr and Mrs Campbell organising the positioning of the little bit of furniture we have, as I enter the new house poor Mr Campbell is trying to move our larder into position with Mother barking out instructions, "Left a bit.. a bit more" she commands, followed by "Stop", an exasperated Mr Campbell sits on the edge of the already successfully positioned sofa bed, " Izzat it ?", he moans ,desperate to return to his own flat, "Ya lazy bastard "Mrs Campbell retorts, "Ye'd hink ye'd dun a days work, gon, bugger aff ya waste a space" she shouts, "Thanks for your help", Mother says as Mr Campbell passes, "Here get yourself a pint of beer" she adds as she hands over some silver coins, "Cheers" Mr Campbell replies, as he looks smugly at his wife,Mrs Campbell looks daggers at him as he quickly heads for the sanctuary of his own flat.

I return to the single end and Father is in the process of putting the last tin of food back in the rogue box, he carefully lifts the box with his hands underneath to avoid a repeat of the earlier incident, as he is just about to make his way next door Mrs Campbell decides to offer some advice "I would haud ra' boatum a' rat box in case the arse faws oot it" she says, "Thanks Mrs Campbell", Father replies sarcastically while shaking his head.

Toffs in the Tenement

There is hardly anything left in the flat apart from a box of cleaning stuff, a couple of dishes in the sink, and Wilhelmina who is still sleeping, Mother and Mrs Campbell look at each other and nod as they move over to the bed recess, they grab a handful of bed clothes in each of their hands and start a mini countdown together," three –two-one they then yank the bed clothes off the bed and poor Wilhelmina is dragged with them , she lets out a highpitched scream as she slides towards the edge of the bed, she is stopped from falling out by Mother who nonchalantly helps a shell shocked and still screaming Wilhelmina to the floor "Sorry Wilhelmina, we forgot you were in there" Mother says as she smiles at her accomplice Mrs Campbell Wilhelmina stamps her feet and heads away in a huff towards the empty space were the settee used to be, she notices its not there and stands totally bewildered, "Your clothes are in the new house", Mother announces, as Wilhelmina storms off in that direction muttering how she hates everything and everybody.

Mother gathers up the coats and Mrs Campbell grabs the blankets and stacks them in the centre of the sheet, she brings the corners of the sheet together and ties them, she then carries the lot through to the new flat, Father arrives with the final items from our single end, and we all head back for one final check, including Mrs Campbell, as we stand there in the middle of the single end the place is totally bare, Father looks , at Mother and says " Onward and upward eh !" as he squeezes her hand, she nods and we turn around to head off to our new house, the sentimental moment is lost on Mrs Campbell who declares in a muffled voice " Thurs hauf a bag a coal in ris bunker",we all turn around to look at her, she is holding open the bunker door with her head right inside the bunker, we all have a good laugh as we leave our single end for the last time.

Toffs in the Tenement

Were o' gon Tae Castlemilk

It's been two weeks now since we moved into our new room and kitchen, and as I lie here in the dark looking out at my new surroundings from the bottom bunk of our new bunk beds, Wilhelmina is fast asleep above me, to my amusement she stirs every now and again from her deep sleep and whinges "Stop calling me Wullie! " to some unknown person who must have annoyed her during the day .

The dying embers of our coal fire still provide enough light to illuminate the room and cast shadows from our recently purchased second hand wardrobe and tallboy onto the freshly laid linoleum, the shadow that has caught my attention on the wall is the one that looks like a giant monster with outstretched arms and spikes coming out of its head, as my eyes follow this monster's shadow on the wall from its   head, past its arms and legs towards the floor, I am relieved to see that the monster is actually Wilhelmina's old Tiny Tears doll with a tiara on it's head, sitting on the floor next to the tallboy.

Suddenly, I notice a shadow on the wall directly opposite the fire that looks like the head of Denis the Menace from the Beano, what is interesting about this shadow though is the fact it's moving, as I turn and look down at the fire, to my surprise, I see a mouse, it is just sitting there in front of the fire preening itself, I am used to seeing mice as we had plenty of them in the single end, but never one that so blatantly didn't care if it was seen, as I lean on my elbow for a more comfortable view, it is joined by another two mice, who appear from the corner near the window, just as this mouse meeting gets underway Wilhelmina stirs above me once again, only this time a Jackie comic she was reading earlier, falls from the top bunk and crashes on the floor, two of the mice scatter back to the corner as soon as the comic hits the floor, but to my amazement one stays exactly where it is, it nonchalantly looks towards the fallen comic, then carries on preening itself while enjoying the heat provided by the dying fire, I decide there and then to call this mouse Samson as it is obviously not afraid of anything.

As I watch Samson busily moving about by the fire, my mind drifts towards tomorrow, when I will be going with Mother to visit Granny and Granda McDonald in Castlemilk, Mother has always told me that my Grandparents moved to their two bedroom home in Castlemilk from a room and kitchen in Partick not long after Mother got married. Father and Wilhelmina are going to visit Grandma and Grandpa Nairn near our old home in the West end.

Wilhelmina loves going "Home" as she calls it, so that she can catch up with her old friends, she also really likes the big detached house Grandma and Grandpa Nairn live in which is near to her favourite place in Glasgow, Byres Rd, she would leave Heron St if she could, and move in permanently with Grandma Nairn without a moments hesitation, but to her dismay and no matter how much she wishes, she has never been asked.

We do this visiting chore at least once a month, with the only difference being I swap with Wilhelmina every month, but, because Mother doesn't like Father's parents and vice versa, they never swap, Mother hasn't spoken to Father's parents since we left the West end two years ago, she blames them for not helping Father at the time of his "trouble" causing Father to sell our big house and move to Bridgeton, and as far as I am aware, both sets of Grandparents only ever met once at the wedding of Mother and Father and even then there was some sort of fallout between the families and they haven't spoken to each other since.

I personally, much prefer going to Castlemilk rather than the West end, Granny and Granda McDonald don't have a lot of money but they are always good fun, and I love listening to their stories about the olden days, how they used to get into the pictures with a penny and a jam jar and how they were that poor when they first got married that when Mother was born she used to sleep in the bottom drawer of a tallboy because they couldn't afford a cot.

Grandma and Grandpa Nairn on the other hand are very well off moneywise, and they are very strict, they hardly give you the time of day when you go to visit, and even when they do it is only to complain about something or scold you for doing something wrong, "children should be seen and not heard ", is Grandma Nairn's favourite saying, and then she will ask "how are you doing at school ?" and when you answer she will say " speak up boy, I cant hear a word you are saying " I wish I could reply "I thought we were to be seen and not heard "

Anyway, as I focus once again on Samson the fire burns out completely, the room becomes very dark, except for the street light outside the bedroom window which penetrates through the gap in the curtains leaving a thin straight line of light on the floor and wall, like a laser beam cutting the room in half.

I can hear the dulcet tones of some drunk men returning home from the Dog Leg pub singing the theme song to the film High Noon as only a Glasgow drunk can, the sound of "Do not fursake me oh ma darlinnnnnnnn",comes wafting up from the dark street below through the gap in my ill fitting bedroom window that wont close properly, they sure know how to hold a note I think to myself.

Samson decides its time to head off and join his friends in the corner, and as I lie back down and pull the duffle coat up around my neck I think to myself "Thank God its Wilhelmina's turn to visit the wicked witch of the West end", this proves to be my last comforting thought before I fall off to sleep.

The next morning I am woken by Wilhelmina's' foot standing on my face as she attempts to climb down from the top bunk, "Ouch! " I screech, as her big toe nearly takes my eye out, this yell of pain frightens the life out of her and she screams as she falls off the ladder, she lands on the floor with a thud, her backside taking the brunt of her fall, she stares at me as if it was my fault for having my face in the way of her foot, she slowly picks herself up off the floor, regains her composure, throws the hair back from her face, smooth's down her nightdress, lifts her nose in the air and marches off towards the room door, she stops briefly to mumble "sorry" before disappearing through the door towards the back room.

As I slowly come to terms with the morning, I throw back my duffle coat duvet and sit on the edge of the bed with my feet on the cold linoleum floor, I am just about to make the effort to get up from the bed when the door opens and Father walks in and stands aimlessly in the middle of the room, this can mean only one thing, someone's using the bucket behind the recess curtains, or as Mother insists on calling it " The En-Suite ".

"Good morning Rupert "Father says as he puffs on his pipe, "Good morning Father" I reply as I pull on my trousers, "Wilhelmina is using the, the," he stutters as he points to the door with his pipe, "lovely morning, eh, what "he stutters again, as he tries desperately to change the subject, he then throws open the curtains and the sunlight floods the room, I am trying to acclimatise my eyes to the light when I hear a shout from Mother of " All clear ", Father strides across the room towards the door then stops suddenly in his tracks, as I look over at him he is peering at something on the floor, "would you look at this " he exclaims, "What" I ask as I walk over towards him, he points to the floor with his pipe and there is Samson brazenly walking across the middle of the room, " Samson " I blurt out, "Who's Samson " father asks, I explain the previous nights activity, and Father agrees not to put down any traps, Father has a smile on his face as he lets me know that Samson can have the run of the place for his cheek. Having successfully secured Samson's safety I get dressed and join the family in the back room for breakfast

Sitting at the breakfast table Mother busily starts to hand out the toast she is making on the two bar electric fire, I notice there are 3 new pots on the table marked Jam, Honey and Butter, as Wilhelmina and me excitedly lift off the lids, licking our lips at the prospect of toast and jam, our hopes are dashed, as the only pot with anything in it is the Butter, the butter I have to say is very tasty, my friend Sammy enviously calls it " Good butter " when he plays in my house, " Aw' we've goat in oor hoose is a block o' Stork " he moans.

Mother buys this particular butter from a shop called Curleys in Main St, I really like Curleys because of the smell, you can smell fresh fruit, cakes etc, and it is always busy with woman gossiping, I laugh at the snippets of conversations I hear " Ah wiz waitin' oan wan last night fur £7 " I heard a lady say, " one what " I asked myself, or the time two ladies were talking and one said to the other " That auldest boy o' mine is rat lazy he's looking fur a pregnant lassie tae marry " this was followed by cackles of laughter, I didn't get it.

Curleys also has a big mirrored pole in the middle of the shop floor, all the kids spend their time hanging on to it and walking round and round while looking at their reflection, there is sawdust on the floor and all the shelves are filled with biscuits, cans, bottles of juice and loads of other goodies that we couldn't afford , behind the counter is a giant block of butter that is cut to order with a wooden spatula and slapped on a piece of greaseproof paper, the butter was never ordered by weight, it was ordered by " a big bit " or " a wee bit ".

Anyway, back at the breakfast table Mother asks "Do you like my new pots?" as she pours tea into Fathers cup, before we can answer she adds "This nice boy came to the door yesterday and told me he was selling them for a children's charity " she then sits the teapot back down on the table and picks up the jam pot and proudly admires it, "Only two bob, and they look like real china," she whispers, Father removes a slice of toast from his mouth, and without lifting his head from his newspaper he asks" What charity was that then dear?", without really paying attention to what Mother was saying, Mother's face now has a puzzled expression as she tries desperately to recall the name of the charity, " Oh I think it was......" before she can finish her sentence she notices Father has lifted the milk jug instead of his tea as he concentrates on his newspaper, "Hubert" Mother barks sternly, as Wilhelmina and me burst out laughing, Father comes to his senses quickly, and noticing the milk jug in his hand, he proclaims apologetically "Sorry dear " as he sheepishly returns the jug to the table and lifts his tea.

"What's so riveting in that newspaper today that you can't take your eyes off it for minute and listen to your wife?" Mother continues, obviously very irritated, Father then insisted on reading the offending passage from the newspaper that had captured his attention, so, in his best BBC newsreader voice he pronounces "Police announced today that they are closing in on the gang who broke into Lewis's department store in Glasgow city centre, a spokesman for Lewis's said "The gang managed to break in through a ground floor window and ransacked the china and glassware department of this famous store", Father pauses for a sip of tea then continues " A spokesman for the Police has asked residents of Glasgow to be on the lookout for anyone suspicious selling cheap china goods or glassware, and to report any incidents immediately to the Police " at this point Mother spurts out her tea and starts coughing, Father jumps up and starts patting her on the back, as Mother regains her composure she seems embarrassed " Right kids, out to play now, I will call you when it is time to leave for Grandma's " she orders, as she snatches the new pots from the table and hides them in the bottom cupboard of the larder, Father looks at us and shrugs his shoulders, he is as confused as us with Mothers erratic behaviour "Out you go " Mother snaps.

Wilhelmina runs straight out the front door as I head for the bedroom to put on my sandshoes, while am in the act of squeezing my foot into my sandshoe, I nearly break my index finger in the process, it gets stuck between the heel of my sandshoe and my ankle as I try desperately to lever my foot inside, there is a knock at the front door, as I continue my struggle, Father opens the front door and shouts " Rupert, its Sammy " as I hop up and down trying release my finger I shout back " I'm coming " just then I hop onto a Tiny Tears doll and fall sideways on to the floor with my finger still stuck, I look up from the floor straight at Sammy who has wandered into the room, "Yer soaks ur too thick " he announces, as he helps me up, obviously he has been in the same predicament at some point, just as I manage to free my now throbbing finger, there is another loud knock at the front door, Father again opens the door and the dulcet tones of our neighbour Mrs Campbell can be heard saying "Oh Mr Nairn, kin ye gie me a hon, rat fat bastard ay' a husband o' mine hiz dun his back in, an' he's bursting furra shi...eh! He needs ra toilet?" she says, correcting herself just in time. "Of course I *kin* give you a *hon* "Father replies with a little bit of Bridgeton brogue, Sammy and I follow Father as he heads for the Campbell's house with Mrs Campbell leading the way, Sammy and I wait at the door as Father goes in to help Mr Campbell, we can see Father entering the front room of the Campbell's just as Mr Campbell shouts "Hurry up wummin, fur Christ's sake, 'am touching cloth here " Mr Campbell notices Father and says "Aw'right Bert, ur ye in tae geeza hon tae ra shitehoose?" Father just nods in agreement , then Mrs Campbell and Father bend over the bed and start to lift Mr Campbell, " Awww' ma effin' back " Mr Campbell moans, as he is hoisted to his feet, the three of them then move toward the front door, Mr Campbell is hunched over in the middle of Father and Mrs Campbell, he stops swearing and moaning long enough to groan " Ma' paper, ma' paper " as he points back at the bed, "I'll get it " I say, as I head into the room.

Now this is the first time I have been in the Campbell's bedroom and the first thing I notice is that it is full of wet washing, the smell is absolutely overwhelming, and as I reach down to pick up the paper from the bed, a little black thing jumps from the bed onto my hand, I pull back quickly, and notice on closer inspection the bed is covered in fleas, there is also a pile of old newspapers, scattered all over the floor and stale blue moulded bread lying on the pillows, empty beer bottles are placed around the room like ornaments and trophies, I also cant help but notice on the bed there is an overflowing ashtray with a partly lit cigarette burning in it, Yuck ! .

I hurriedly leave to deliver the paper to Mr Campbell but by the time I catch up with them on the toilet landing, Sammy is holding open the door and Father and Mrs Campbell are trying to reverse Mr Campbell into the toilet, he is in the process of lifting up his dirty striped nightgown, when Father stutters " Eh! Can you possibly wait until I've gone before you do that?" Mr Campbell nods at Father and is then gently lowered onto the toilet, it was a bit like lowering a bull elephant onto a child's potty; As Father closes the door an exhausted Mrs Campbell gasps," Thanks fur yer help Mr Nairn" she takes another breath and continues "He's been like rat furra week noo, am bloody scunnered wi' it so ah 'um".

As they head back up the stairs. Sammy and I are just about to head down the stairs when we hear what sounds like one hundred whoopee cushions going off at the same time in the toilet, followed by the relieved voice of Mr Campbell sighing "Ahhhhhhh! Ya dancer!", we quickly head down the stairs being chased by a horrendous smell, and just as we reach the bottom stair we can hear Mr Campbell moan "Ya wee bastard! Y'er away wi' ma paper" Sammy looks at me, as I notice I am still holding the paper I had fetched for Mr Campbell," Come back wi' ma' paper ya wee bugger" Mr

Campbell shouts again, I quickly drop the evidence on the bottom stair and we run out the close laughing.

Half an hour later, Sammy and I are sitting on the pavement outside my close reading old copies of the Beezer and the Topper comics that we found in the street, when Wilhelmina comes out of our close with father, "See you later Rupert " Father says, "we're off to Grandpa Nairn's' " he continues as he heads off down Heron St towards Dalmarnock Rd , just then Mother leans out of our window about ten feet above me and Sammy and shouts " Ruuupeeeert " at the top of her voice," I'm down here Mother " I say quietly as she exclaims " Oh,right, well it's time to get ready for Granny Mc Donald's " she adds, I say goodbye to Sammy and head up the stair to get my coat.

Mother locks the door and we head down the stair, as we pass the toilet landing we can hear Mr Campbell shouting from the toilet " Ina, Ina am dun, geeza hon " he begs " Ina " he screams, on hearing Mr Campbell's pleas for help Mother holds her index finger up to her pursed lips indicating to me not to say anything as she escorts me down the stairs and we march towards Dalmarnock rd at the speed of light, Mother has no intention of getting involved in the palaver of returning Mr Campbell to his house.

Just as we are approaching Dalmarnock rd we have one last hurdle to overcome, Mrs McKay has spotted us and as we pass her window she asks "going somewhere nice Mrs Nairn?" Mother stops and looks straight at Mrs Mc Kay "Just going to my mothers " Mother replies in a matter of fact manner, "That's nice "continues Mrs Mc Kay with fake sincerity, "by ra way, did ye buy anything aff rat guy that wiz gon roon ra doors yisterday selling stuff?" she quizzes, "Ah telt him to bugger aff coz ah knew he wiz up tae nae good " she says indignantly, Mother starts to blush as she lifts her nose in the air and replies " I don't buy from door to door salespeople Mrs McKay" as we swiftly carry on to the relative safety of Dalmarnock Rd.

"See rat bloody wummin" Mother mutters under her breath, not realising that I can hear her, as we head along Dalmarnock Rd towards Woolworths and the number 46 bus stop.

When we arrive at the bus stop outside Woolworths Mother announces "Wait here Rupert, I am just going to the Countdown for a packet of biscuits " The Countdown is the first Asian shop I have ever seen and is directly opposite Woolworths next to Lennox's sweet shop and the Dominion pub, it sells all sorts of groceries etc , a bit like Curleys on Main st, as Mother crosses the road I am left standing at the bus stop with two old woman for company, with mouths on them like sewers, I overhear one saying to the other " Ah knew the stuff was knocked aff so ah telt him tae get tae f.." just in the nick of time Mother arrives back " Custard creams " she declares waving the packet in front of me, before putting them in a Marks and Spencer's bag I hadn't noticed she was carrying .

The number 46 bus turned the corner from Bridgeton Toll at the Cactus pub and hurtled towards us, the two old woman rush forward to put their hands out as the bus approaches the bus stop, I have noticed a young man who is hanging from the pole at the entrance of the bus in readiness to get off, and as the bus is slowing down to stop, he tries to show off by jumping off while the bus is still moving, he has obviously mis-judged the speed and as his feet hit the ground about 15 feet from the bus stop, he picks up speed and is sent flying into the two old woman, knocking them down like skittles, he then bounces off the bus stop and lands flat on his face on top of a dozen eggs from one of the woman's bags , as Mother and I help the two old women to their feet the young man is slowly getting to his feet with the eggs running down his face covering his now bright red cheeks, " Ya bammy bastard " one old woman shouts at the young man as she rises gingerly to her feet, " Yiv smashed o' ma eggs ya eejit " shouts the other woman as she looks at the mushy mess that used to be her bag of groceries, the young man sheepishly tries to help gather up all the women's belongings while apologising at the same time, but the old women were having none of it, " Go'n bugger aff" shouts old woman number two as she swings the remnants of her bag of groceries at the young mans head, but the young man ducks and the bag hits old woman number one with a dull mushy thud, right across her face which sends her spinning and then she falls on her backside, by this time a small crowd has gathered and as the old women help each other the young man takes the opportunity to make a quick getaway, after some calm has been restored we help the old ladies on to the bus, and as they sit down together to discuss the incident there is a shout of " Oh! Ma arse", from old woman number one as she descends on to the seat.

As the bus moves away the young conductress comes over to us "Fares please "she shouts to no-one in particular, "One adult and one child to Castlemilk please " Mother states with purpose, in her poshest voice, as she holds out her hand with the money, " Weryegon " comes the reply from the young conductress, " Pardon,? " Mother retorts, "Wer...Ur...Ye...Gon," the conductress repeats in a slow drawl, the same way you would talk to an old deaf person; slightly taken aback by this response Mother replies in the same slow drawl "My... Mothers...house... " at that moment everyone round about us starts to snigger, the conductress shakes her head and tries again " Naw , were ur ye gon in Castlemilk , so ah know whit tae charge ye " she asks, " Oh " says Mother, " Sorry, Machrie Rd " she mutters sheepishly,

Toffs in the Tenement

"That'll be 9d " announces the conductress, as she pushes down on her ticket machine twice producing the tickets and handing them to Mother.

By this time we are approaching Dalmarnock Bridge just before Farmeloan Rd when the bus pulls in at a bus stop, on comes a small woman carrying about five bags of groceries, she squeezes into the space right beside Mother, who is not best pleased with the situation, she then places her bags on the floor and sighs, she then turns to Mother and proclaims "See me, rat's me fae yisterday " A puzzled expression appears on Mothers face and is still there when the woman continues " Av' no' stoaped neerar a huv " , Mother nods as if she understands and tries to shift along the seat a bit.

We are now approaching Rutherglen Main St, and as we turn into Main St opposite Chapmans pub the bus stops again, Mother looks to see who is getting on the bus and exclaims under her breath "Oh No!" I look over to see the reason for the "Oh No!" Just in time to see a drunk man trying to navigate the one step up onto the platform at the entrance to the bus, "Hullorerr Hen "he says to the conductress, she looks totally unimpressed with his greeting and retorts " Sit oan yer arse and geez peace " the drunk man staggers on to the bus and is trying to find a seat when the bus moves off, this motion sends him flying face first into Mother, who is totally horrified, with the drunk man's face about two inches from Mothers he looks her right in the eye and says " ye awrite rer doll ?", Mother screws up her face and sternly answers " Go away you disgusting little man ", On hearing this response the drunk man straightens himself up as best he can, he stares at Mother and then starts to walk down the aisle of the bus towards a vacant seat, he stops at a young man sitting at the edge of the aisle, leans over, puts his hand on the young man's shoulder and declares in a loud voice " Who shoved a brush up her arse ?", motioning his head towards Mother, the young man tries not to laugh as the drunk man sits opposite him and opens a half bottle of whisky giggling with delight at his quip, Mother looks daggers in his direction and then at the young man , who suddenly straightens his face and faces the front.

At this point we are passing the Odeon cinema and turn left into Mill St and continue past the Wallace bar towards the Mill Hotel, just after the Mill Hotel the bus stops outside the cemetery, the drunk man starts to make the effort to get off, and as he staggers towards Mother enroute to the exit, he looks directly at her and growls "It's awrite ya torn faced witch 'am getting' aff", To my surprise Mother just smiles, but then as the drunk man draws level with us Mother ever so slightly sticks out her foot, the drunk falls face first in the aisle sending his half bottle bouncing down the bus and straight onto the street, smashing into a thousand pieces, he then tries to grab a handrail and misses completely sending his arm onto the small woman's bags of groceries, she picks up her handbag with both hands and smashes it on the drunk's head shouting " Watch whit yer daen av' goat eggs in rer ya clown ", The drunk man continued to crawl towards the exit with the small woman repeatedly hitting him over the head "Geeza brek" he screams before crawling off the bus, he stands up holding his head just as the bus moves off, he fixes his glare on Mother who just smiles at him with a smile that says that will teach you not to mess with me.

We then head down Croftfoot Rd and turn left at St Bartholomew's school into Castlemilk Drive, as Mother and I prepare to get off, the bus pulls in at Machrie Rd and I jump off followed by Mother who looks at the conductress and mouths the words "thank you" as she steps off the bus, the conductress doesn't reply or even acknowledge Mother's pleasantry as she presses the red button which rings the bell and lets the driver know he can move off.

"Peasant ", Mother sneers as she sorts her bags and we head up Machrie Rd towards Machrie Drive, about one hundred yards along Machrie Rd sits Alec's ice cream van, I stop and give Mother my best begging face hoping for a twin top cone, she doesn't even break stride and marches on past Alec's van, as we pass the small row of shops on Machrie Rd, I try again to no avail and we keep on going past the chip shop, I really love this part of Machrie Rd as the view is spectacular , you can see all over Glasgow , including all the football stadiums Celtic, Rangers, Clyde, Hampden, also all the new fancy tower blocks that are being built.

We reach Machrie Drive and walk through the backcourt to Granny McDonalds house at number 20, as we climb the stairs I can hear Granny's voice shouting "They're here" ,she must have seen us from her kitchen window, "Rupert" she screeches with her arms outstretched, I'm now resigned to the fact I am going to receive a slobbery Granny kiss and a hug that would do a grizzly bear proud, "Granny", I say in a half hearted manner copying the outstretched hands routine as she charges towards me with her big chest bouncing about like lethal weapons, after a hug that Mick Mc Manus would have submitted to, and a kiss on the forehead that revealed she really needs to shave her upper lip, she releases her grip and I manage to escape inside the house.

I walk into the living room just in time to see Granda putting the T.V. section of the Daily Record up against the living room window, the reason for this strange custom was to inform the local bookie that he wished to place a bet that day on the horses, I was warned by Granda McDonald long ago never to tell anyone outside the house of this arrangement as it wasn't a particularly legal practice.

"Granda", I shout, "Rupert", Granda replies as he marches towards me and does the same pretend boxing routine he always does every time I see him, followed by the inevitable ruffling of my hair, "My, my, look at ra size o' you", he continues, as he holds me by the shoulders while looking me up and down, "Ur ye married yit", he asks jokingly, as we both start to laugh we are joined by Mother and Granny who enter the living room with their arms linked together, Granny leads Mother over to the table were she has made sandwiches and tea, "Right everybody sit doon an ah'll mask ra' tea", she orders, as she heads off into the kitchen.

While Granny is in the kitchen Mother and Granda are in deep conversation at the table, so I decide to follow Granny into the kitchen, the first thing I notice is piles of washing in her double sink, she has a big deep sink and a smaller sink, in the middle of both sinks is a big mangle, this is two rollers and a handle and is used for wringing and squeezing the water out of the wet washing. " Will ye give me hand to wring the rest of that washing Rupert " Granny asks, as she lifts a full teapot off the gas cooker and heads towards the living room, I reluctantly nod my head behind her back as I follow her carrying the milk jug, , I can still remember the last time I was asked to do this chore, when I tried to wring the water out of a jumper and couldn't move the handle of the mangle, I was left hanging from the handle with both feet off the floor and it still wouldn't budge, Granny then came in, and on noticing my predicament, she shook her head from side to side and laughed, I was then unceremoniously lifted out of the way as she rolled up her sleeves, grabbed hold of the handle and turned it with one hand, while catching the washing as it passed through the rollers with the other hand, "Ye better start eating yer porridge", she quipped sarcastically, as I was swiftly demoted to folding duties.

Just as we joined Granda and Mother at the table there was a loud banging on the front door and a booming voice could be heard all through the close shouting " Cooooaallll ", Granny looked at me as she poured the tea through a strainer into a cup, "Will ye lift the snib in the bunker fur ra coalman Rupert?", I headed off down the hall to the coal bunker at the front door, I open the door and carefully lean over to the small wooden window inside the bunker and release the lock, just then the small window flies open and this big black face appears frightening the life out of me, as I jump back I tumble over the small wooden guard that keeps the coal from falling out the bunker and into the hall, and end up on my backside on the hall floor, "How many bags dae ye want?" the coalman asks as he takes the rolled up cigarette out of his mouth, I am just recovering from the shock when Granny shouts from the living room "Jist wan", the coalman heads off and Granny shouts again " Ur ye alright there Rupert?", I rise to my feet and notice I am missing a shoe as I reply "I'm fine", I can see my shoe is sitting on top of the little coal left in the bunker so I reach in to retrieve it, as I lift up my shoe I hear an almighty crash as a full bag of coal is deposited in the bunker by the coalman, once again I am sent flying backwards onto my backside, after the dirt and dust has settled I am left holding the shoe but still coughing and spluttering.

I put my shoe on ,reach in and lock the small window inside the coal bunker, close the bunker door and head back into the living room, " RUPERT" Mother screams, as I enter the room, Granny and Granda start sniggering before Granda exclaims " Look its Al Jolsen" Granny starts to laugh out loud as Granda starts waving both hands at the side of his face, singing " Mammeee, Mammeee" Mother draws him a look as she grabs my arm and escorts me toward the bathroom, in the bathroom mirror I can see the reason for the hilarity, I look like a miniature black and white minstrel off the television, as Mother gets to work cleaning my now removed shirt, I make a start on my face and hands, while all the time thinking " Who's Al Jolsen?".

After I have scrubbed the coal dust from my face, and my shirt has been duly returned in an acceptable condition, I ask if I go out to play, a "Mammy inspection" follows before I am given the required affirmative permission and off I go outside.

I am standing at Granny's close when I notice a group of men across at the tree stump on the grass triangle opposite Granny's house, one is sitting on the tree stump and the others are standing in line playing some sort of game, I slowly make my way over for a closer look as I get nearer I can hear one man say to the other "Ur you playing' wi' a Vikki?", the other man looks at his hand and answers " Aye, ah polished it wi' duraglit this mornin' ".
After watching the men for about 2 hours I learned that they were playing a game called Moashie, this involved 3 holes about 4 inches diameter, dug into the ground, about six feet apart in a straight line, the men stood in a line at the bottom hole, as if they were in the queue at the post office, and one at a time threw a penny at the top hole, missing out the middle hole, if they all missed the hole and one person got his penny in first time he would tap the other pennies around the hole and keep them, if more than one person got his penny in the hole the last one in kept the money, now if they all missed, the nearest to the hole went first and threw his penny to the middle hole, and then the bottom hole, then the middle again, till he found himself back at the top hole, if he managed to complete this task in one go without missing a hole the other men paid him a penny each.

Toffs in the Tenement

I also discovered that a "Vikki" was a penny with Queen Victoria on it, some of the men would polish this penny to make it more shiny and slippery, they would use this penny all the time and if they lost they would pay the victor with a normal penny from their pocket rather than part with their "Lucky Penny", I was absolutely fascinated by this game, and the fact that grown men were playing it.

The language used while playing moashie was rather vociferous, things like "Ma penny izza baw hair nearer than yoorz" and "It wisnae your shot ya bastard" were common remarks during a game, one man, who looked like Hen Broon out of the Broons, had to leave when his son arrived breathless and informed him " Ma Maw's daen her nut, yer dinner's been ready fur ages", I have never seen a man walking that fast without actually running, his friends started shouting derogatory remarks using mock voices, things like " Yer dinners ready Charlie, ye better hurry up" and " Haw Charlie, Yer dinners in the dug" followed by one comedian shouting " his dinner *is* ra dug, ah won a' his money" as he is joined in a chorus of laughter by the rest of the men.

At this point I was sniggering as well at poor Charlie's expense, when out the corner of my eye I spotted Mother at the mouth of Granny's close, her head was moving like the light on a lighthouse looking for me, I jumped to my feet and ran as fast as i could towards the close, I arrived just as Mother had taken a deep breath and was about to shout my name, God knows what the men would have done had she shouted *"Rupert"*, Mother informed me we were heading home and I said my goodbyes to Granda and Granny Mc Donald, Granda then told me he would see me tomorrow as him and Granny were coming to see our new flat in Heron St.

Toffs in the Tenement

Ra' In-Laws Ur Coming

Later on, as we get off the 46 bus at the Dominion Pub near Bridgeton Cross, we cross the road and start walking towards Heron St, suddenly a voice behind us shouts "Clarissa" and as we turn around we spot Father and Wilhelmina passing Woolworths making their way towards us.

As we all walk up Heron St towards our close, Wilhelmina prattles on about seeing her old friends in the West end and how fabulous Grandfather Nairn's house is., Never once does she ask about Granny or Granda Mc Donald much to my chagrin. Father is talking excitedly but not actually saying anything, much to the frustration of Mother.

When we enter our flat Mother has had enough, "Hubert" she says abruptly as she starts to remove her coat, "Spit it out, what happened at your Fathers" she demands, as she hands him her coat and marches into the back room. Father hangs up her coat at the third attempt, and follows her into the back room. "Well nothing really" he stutters as he enters the room, "But" he continues, by this time Mother is losing patience as she fills the kettle at the sink, "But What", Mother asks sharply, as she lifts a cup out of the cupboard "Well ,there is something going on" Father continues, "Because my parents are coming to see us tomorrow and ..." before he can say anything else there is a smashing sound as the cup Mother is holding crashes to the floor and breaks into a thousand pieces, Mother is standing motionless for a few seconds before looking at me and then at Father still holding her hand as if the cup is still there, "Are you okay Clarissa?", Father asks, as he runs over to Mother "What's wrong, your face has turned pure white, as if you have seen a ghost?", Father continues ,as he leads Mother to the couch and sits her down, Mother regains her composure, and looking at Father says in a whisper "My parents are coming too", on hearing this Father, who is bent down beside Mother at the side of the couch, falls backwards and sits on the broken glass from the cup Mother dropped, " Ouch ! My backside", he exclaims, as he jumps up and tries to brush off the small pieces of shattered glass that are now lodged in his posterior, " What do you mean?", he shouts at Mother, while continuing to dance about like a red Indian doing a rain dance, "Your parents are coming here?, to this house?, tomorrow?, at the same time as my parents?", he enquires while slapping the glass from his behind, "Oh dear, this is not good", he says worriedly, "I agree", replies Mother, " No! I think my bums bleeding", Father retorts, "Never mind yer bleeding bum" Mother replies angrily, "What are we going to do about our parents?", she ponders, as she bites hard on her bottom lip with a look of sheer panic on her face.

An hour later as we sit in the back room, Mother is silently preparing our supper, and Father is sitting on a bundle of washing to protect his now tender backside. There is a knock at the door, "See who it is Rupert?", Father asks. I make my way to the door, but before I can reach it the front door opens and in walks Mrs Campbell shouting "YooHoo! Ur ye in Mrs Nairn?". She carries on and enters the back room before anyone can answer, "Oh there yur there, Mrs Nairn", she exclaims as she notices Mother at the sink, "Kin ah' borrow a wee tait mulk aff ye ,it's fur ma man's tea?", Mother nods and replies "Of course you can Mrs Campbell", as she pours some milk into a cup, Mrs Campbell has noticed Father sitting on the bundle of washing by this time and comments "They Duke o'Argylls are murder, int they?", "Sorry" Father retorts not understanding what Mrs Campbell means " Fur Christ's sake ur ye deaf as well as daft", she says sarcastically, "Ah Said, they piles ur murder, int they?", she repeats slowly pointing in the direction of the washing under Fathers rear end. "Oh right, I see" says Father as the penny drops, "No, No, No, its not haemorrhoids" replies Father, "Ah never says it wiz hemorwotsits, ah said it wiz piles" she fires back indignantly shaking her head. "ya smug Bastard" she mutters under her breath. "Here's your milk Mrs Campbell", Mother interrupts, handing over the cup, and escorting Mrs Campbell off the premises, " Could you do me a small favour ?", Mother asks Mrs Campbell as she opens the front door. I could then hear them whispering, this continued onto the landing, with Mother and Mrs Campbell whispering for another ten minutes.

"What was that all about ?", asks Father on Mother's return, "Never you mind", Mother replies, followed by "Right kids time for bed, we have all got a big day tomorrow".

Toffs in the Tenement

As I lie in bed, Wilhelmina is fast asleep above me in the top bunk, her foot sticking out the bed just far enough for me to try and hit it with elastic bands, I start to think about the next day, and a multitude of questions pop into my head, Questions like ,what was going to happen when both sets of grandparents met?, what did Grandfather Nairn want to tell us?, Why were Mother and Father so apprehensive about the visit?, and what were Mother and Mrs Campbell whispering about?, and finally, who the hell was Al Jolsen?, just as I pondered these issues I scored a direct hit with an elastic band on Wilhelmina's foot, and she let out a loud groan, this was my signal to get to sleep fast.

The next morning, I go round to see if Sammy wants to come out to play, I knock on Sammy's door and his mother answers, "Is Sammy coming out to play?", I ask, "He's already oot" his mother replies, "Listen Rupert, he wiz at ra swimmin' yisterday wi' his Da, an he goat a draught in his ear", she continues, "He kin hardly hear any'hing oot his left ear, an' he will be like rat until it pops" she tells me, "Jist in case yer wondering why he keeps saying "Whit" o' ra time", she says with a smile on her face "He said he wiz gon tae Walters fur sweeties", she concludes as she closes the door.

I leave Sammy's close and head for Walters, as I am walking down Heron St near the Dog Leg pub, Sammy comes round the corner with sweeties in one hand, and his other hand slapping his ear trying to get it to pop, as I reach Sammy he groans "Ma' ear's blocked", "I know, your Mother told me", I answer loudly, "Ah kin hardly hear anyfing", he adds as he sticks a finger in his ear and moves it vigorously from side to side, "Are your lugs alright?", I ask sympathetically, On hearing my question Sammy jumps back and starts hopping on one foot, "What are you doing?", I ask, as I grab his arm, Sammy looks at me right in the eye and says " Ah thought ye said, "there's a dugs shite", we both start to laugh, as we head back down Heron St and I fill Sammy in with the story of my Grandparents expected visit in about an hours time.

When we reach my close at No 43 we bump into Father who is in the process of putting on his jacket and rushing out of the close, he spots me and Sammy and slides to halt like a Keystone Kop, "Ah! Rupert there you are" he exclaims as he finishes buttoning his jacket , "I am off to buy some biscuits", he declares, he then pulls the bottom of his jacket with both hands, straightens his tie, takes a deep breath and asks "Abernethy ok?", I nod my approval as heads off down Heron St towards Dalmarnock Rd, as I turn to Sammy he has a puzzled expression on his face, " Is yer Da' gon tae Aberfeldy ?" he asks, I smile as I shake my head to indicate "No" and motion with my head for Sammy to follow me.

Toffs in the Tenement

Sammy and I make our way through my close to the backcourt, we fight our way through the washing hanging on the clothes lines and climb on top of the brick shed that houses the rubbish bins, from our new vantage point we have a superb view across the Booly to London Rd, Dalmarnock Rd and the backcourts of wee Heron St to the right. " Look", shouts Sammy, pointing to the corner of the Booly where big Heron St meets wee Heron St at the back of the Dog leg pub. At this point there is a big slide about 40 feet long from the top of the Booly to the ground below, the grass on this section of the hill has been worn away by hundreds of kids sliding down the hill on anything they could sit on , leaving only a smooth sandy surface and thousands of small loose stones. "There's naebody oan ra' slide", Sammy exclaims.

Now this is a truly unique situation as there is usually somebody on the slide and me and Sammy have never been able to have a go. "If you want a shot, let's go", I say to Sammy, who replies "Naw! Ah don't want a' shot o' yer Lego, I want tae go oan ra slide", he moans, "Come on", I say, pulling him towards the slide. We run along the 12 inch thick brick wall that separates the backcourts of Heron St with the Booly, although there is a 10 foot drop on either side of the wall this only adds to the adventure. When we reach the end of the wall level with the slide, I sit down on the wall, Sammy joins me and asks" Ur we gonny dreepit or jump?", I had already decided to "Dreepit" as Sammy put it, and lower myself over the edge of the wall and hold on with my fingers, at this point my feet are still about 4 feet from the ground, Sammy does the same and as we look at each other we start to count backwards from three. "Three, Two, One", we chant in unison, and on reaching 'one' we both let go, as we hit the ground we fall backwards onto the grass laughing.

Looking down the slide it looks even bigger than before, the old bashed metal road sign that is used for sitting on is at the bottom of the slide, "Ah'll get it", Sammy screams as he hurtles himself down the hill on foot, halfway down he loses his balance and falls backwards continuing his journey to the bottom on his back, screaming with delight at the whole experience.

As the dust settles I can just about make out the silhouette of Sammy who is standing triumphantly holding the metal sign above his head. He runs back up the hill pulling the sign behind him, and we balance it near the edge of the slide, I get on first and Sammy sits behind me with his hands locked around my waist, we rock back and forth moving the sign nearer and nearer the edge, "Wait", shouts Sammy as he puts his finger in his ear and after a couple of seconds he shouts excitedly " Gon ya dancer, ma ear's popped", he re clasps his hands around my waist and with one last almighty forward movement we lurch over the edge and hurtle down the slide with dust and stones flying through the air, and Sammy and me squealing with delight, we pick up even more speed, and it's at this point the thought occurs to me that we don't know how to stop this thing. The ground below is getting rapidly nearer and Sammy has just had the same thought , the pitch of his squealing has changed to fear, I pull the edge of the sign in a vain attempt to stop but only succeed in tipping us over and we go sprawling off the sign and hurtling down the hill on our backs closely followed by the sign we should be sitting on.

We hit the bottom of the hill with a thud and continue spinning and rolling along the ground grinding to a halt just before a piece of ground covered in broken glass, our sign clatters into the both of us and settles on top of Sammy, we slowly regain our composure and stand up , I point at Sammy and start laughing and he in turn points at me laughing heartily, as we are both covered in dust and dirt with scraped knees and knuckles, "Lets dae it again", we excitedly say at the same time. Just then I hear Jamie McCabe shouting from the top of the hill "Haw bawheid, yer Maw wants ye", I assume he means me and reluctantly say cheerio to Sammy, "Bring ra' sign wi' ye ya bampots", Jamie shouts, to rub salt in the wound.

A few minutes later I am standing outside our flat trying to rub off the dirt from my knees when the door opens and Mother lets out a shriek "Rupert" look at the state of you", before I can proclaim my innocence I am dragged into the backroom and stripped down to my underwear, after Mother is finished attacking me with soap and a wet cloth, I am ushered into the bedroom and ordered to put on clean clothes and report back for inspection before my Grandparents arrive.

While I am getting dressed there is a knock at the front door, Mother answers the door but I can't hear who it is, all I hear is mumbled voices. After I am dressed I pick up the comb and head toward the back room for inspection. "Can you comb my hair?", I ask as I open the door, I am stopped in my tracks by the sight of Mrs Campbell standing there looking shiny and clean, with a brand new white apron and shiny shoes, she also had a series of kirbies in her hair that Mother was sorting. "There that looks lovely Mrs Campbell, now you know what to do, don't you?" she asks, "Aye aye, jist remember ma money", Mrs Campbell retorts.

Mother moves over to the sink and starts cleaning cups while I sit on the couch and stare at Mrs Campbell, she looks straight at me and whispers "whit ye looking at ya wee shite", I quickly remove my gaze and pretend to look at the ceiling, just then Father comes in and upon noticing Mrs Campbell lets out a sarcastic "wolf whistle", followed by "Mrs Campbell don't you look, er, different?", he gushes, "Aye awright ya sarky bastart" she responds sharply.

"Can I wait downstairs?" I ask Mother, "Go on then, but don't get a mark on you", she answers sternly. Just as I reach the front of the close I look down the street and see Granny and Granda Mc Donald walking towards me, I run the 20 yards or so towards them and Granny opens her arms, "Oh no!", I think to myself ,sure enough she grabs me in a bear hug and plants a slobbery kiss on my forehead, she just releases her grip in time for Granda to start his boxing routine, I guide them up to the flat ,when the kissing and hugging starts with Mother and Father I decide to head back downstairs, as I leave the flat I nearly run into Mr Campbell who has a paper under his arm, to my surprise he walks past the toilet and carries on downstairs and out the close heading up towards the Dog Leg pub, I am still watching him when I hear the horn of a car, as I look to my right there is a big black car at the bottom of the street just passing a group of children playing rounders, they drop their bat and ball and start to follow the car up the street towards me. Sure enough it was Grandfather Nairn in his prized black Sunbeam mark 3 motor car, he was moving slowly up the street looking at the numbers on the closes', suddenly he spots me and speeds up leaving the gang of children in his wake.

As he stops outside my close the children catch up and surround the car, "Is it the Queen?", one child asks, "Naw its ra Pope" announces another, "Who's deed?" asks the smallest child, as he catches up with the rest. Suddenly the drivers' door opens and out comes Grandfather Nairn, he closes the door and puts on his bowler hat, he always reminds me of Winston Churchill, with his long black coat and bowler hat, he then places a black brolly over his arm and walks round to the passenger side of the car where he opens the door and helps Grandmother out, who as usual looks resplendent in her fur coat and hat. "Is that a deed dug oan her heed?" says one of the children, much to the amusement of the rest, but not Grandfather who growls, "Go on, move along there", which was enough to send the group of children running off.

Turning his attention to me he nods and grumbles " Hello Rupert", as he leads Grandmother inside the close, Grandmother hasn't even said hello yet when she screws up her nose and asks "What is that smell?", "We are on the first floor", I say totally ignoring Grandmothers question " Lead on Rupert", Grandfather orders pointing inside the close with his brolly.

When we reach the toilet landing I declare "That's the toilet for all of us on this floor", as we continue up the stairs, Grandmother shakes her head at the thought and looks at Grandfather, He just nods again and leads her up the stairs to our flat. I open the door to announce their arrival, first to respond is

Toffs in the Tenement

Father who runs through to the front door to greet them, it turns out that they haven't yet told the McDonalds that the Nairn's were visiting as well. "Mother, Father, glad you could come", he gushes as he helps them off with their coats, meanwhile I have sat down on the couch as Granny McDonald innocently asks Mother "Is rat somebody else come tae visit ye as well?".

At this point the blood has drained from Mother's face, and small beads of sweat have formed on her forehead, "Are ye o.k.?" asks Granda, before she can answer the living room door opens and in walks... Wilhelmina, Mother is just about to let out a sigh of relief when Wilhelmina announces "What are Grandfather and Grandmother Nairn doing in the hall?", Mother winces as the words leave Wilhelmina's lips as she waits for the forthcoming shouting match. "Oh good, there here", Granny McDonald says calmly, Mother looks at her totally puzzled as Grandfather Nairn enters the room and heads straight over to Granny and Granda, he stretches out his hand and shakes both of them warmly by the hand saying "Maggie, Jock, good to see you again" Mother and Father are totally dumbfounded at this, so was I, apart from the courteous greeting I never knew Granny and Granda's first names' were Maggie and Jock.

Everyone sits down and Mother asks "What's going on?", Grandmother Nairn suggests we all have a cup of tea as Grandfather has an announcement to make, everyone drinks their tea and Mrs Campbell walks around with a tray of little triangle sandwiches and Abernethy biscuits, Grandfather Nairn stands up and taps his chipped cup with a teaspoon, everyone falls silent except Mrs Campbell who scolds Grandfather by saying "Ho you watch ra good cups", he stares at her as he is not used to being spoken like that, but softens his glare and says "Sorry". "Aye ye bloody no better", she retorts.

Everyone in the room now has their eyes fixed firmly on Grandfather Nairn as he stands in front of the fireplace, Mother and Father are sitting on the couch holding hands beside Grandmother, me and Wilhelmina are on the floor, and Granny and Granda are sitting on the two dining chairs.

"Fur Christ sake Hurry up wull ye, av goat ma mans dinner tae put oan?", moans Mrs Campbell, Grandfather straightens up and once again, clears his throat with a nervous cough and glares at Mrs Campbell, "So, you are probably wondering what is going on?", he begins, everybody nods their heads, " Three weeks ago I wrote a letter to Maggie and Jock asking them to meet me in Glasgow city centre for lunch, I'm not getting any younger and thought it was about time we sorted out our differences, they kindly agreed, after all Maggie was my secretary for 15 years and a very good one at that", Wilhelmina looks at me and mouths the words "I didnt know that" "Nor me", I mouth back, Grandfather continues as he looks at Father " Just about the time you set a date for your wedding Jock thought Maggie and me were eh,em" "Winchin", Granda interrupts, "Yes quite" Grandfather continues, "Anyway, Jock approached me at your wedding after the first dance to confirm his thoughts and , well lets just say we fell out. During that time I was taking my anger out on Hubert for wanting to marry Maggie's daughter Clarissa, and even refused to pay for the wedding" "I didn't know that" Mother says, "Well its true, I'm sorry Clarissa, I have just found out that Hubert borrowed the money for the wedding from an unscrupulous source and spent the next 8 years trying to pay it back" "Is this true Hubert ?", Mother asks, Father sheepishly nods his head, "It wasn't Hubert's fault Clarissa, he was only doing his best, it was my fault for not helping", Grandfather adds, " When young Wilhelmina started Private school and then Rupert the pressure became too much and the people Hubert owed the money to applied extreme pressure on him to keep up his payments and, in a moment of desperation he took fifty pounds from the bank were he worked to keep these despicable people happy, I was shocked, disgusted and embarressed when the auditors found out, but I didn't know or wouldn't listen to Hubert's excuses and shunned him, I let the board tell Hubert he would never work in a bank again, and sack him. I refused to help when he lost his home and had to move here to Heron St, I let my grandchildren be moved from their school, and I watched as he struggled to get a job".

"Ya bad old bastard", Mrs Campbell scowls, Grandfather still looks shocked when Father suggests "Its ok, were managing fine", "No Hubert, its not ok,", he continues "And that's why.. I have a new job for you, you can start in the TSB bank at Bridgeton Cross as assistant manager, the manager is a good friend of mine and he will bring you up to date with what is required, he is retiring next year and you will fill his position when he goes, is that ok.. SON?", Father slumps back on the couch as Wilhelmina jumps up and down screaming her delight, Mother looks at Father with tears in her eyes and says " You always believed you would do it, didn't you?", "Ya jammy Bastards" is Mrs Campbell's input, as all my Grandparents give each other a hug.

The next morning Wilhelmina and I join Mother at the breakfast table, Father has already went out and as Mother puts our toast on the fire, Wilhelmina is the only one with a smile on her face, "Can I skip breakfast please?", Wilhelmina asks "I want to tell my friends our good news", she continues, Mother nods and Wilhelmina skips out the door singing and dancing a jig of joy.

"How do you feel about the news Rupert?" Mother asks, after thinking for a minute I reply "I don't really know, I am happy for Father, and you of course, but I will miss Sammy, and seeing Father every day, and I will also miss Mrs campbell", Mother stops what she is doing and gazes out the window at the sink, deep in thought. The silence is broken when Father comes bounding in through the front door, "Well?" Mother asks, Father throws off his coat and sits down, "That's it sorted", he announces, "That's what sorted?" I ask, "You tell him", Mother says to Father, "Well Rupert, we have decided to stay here, well not here exactly, but stay in Bridgeton", "What about your new job?", I ask with a confused expression on my face,"Oh! I am still taking the job, but your Grandfather pulled a few strings with the council and we will be moving to the brand new high flats being built in Ruby St, so you don't need to change school, and you can still see Sammy".Out the corner of eye I notice Mrs Campbell has walked through our front door holding an empty cup she borrowed yesterday, and has been standing in the hall listening to all this.

"I would have missed Mrs Campbell as well", Mother adds,as she places a slice of toast in front of me, "Ah should bloody well think so", Mrs Campbell announces as she walks in the room, and we all start laughing. Just then we can hear the dulcet tones of Wilhelmina singing as she comes up the stairs, we all look at each other, and in unison cry out "Oh No!"

THE END

Available soon   **The Toffs in the Towerblock**

Toffs in the Tenement

Toffs in the Tenement

Printed in Poland
by Amazon Fulfillment
Poland Sp. z o.o., Wrocław